ALL THE LIES THEY DID NOT TELL

ALL THE LIES THEY DID NOT TELL

THE TRUE STORY OF SATANIC PANIC IN AN ITALIAN COMMUNITY

PABLO TRINCIA

TRANSLATED BY ELETTRA PAULETTO

Author's Note: nothing in this book was dramatized in any way. Certain names have been changed.

Previously published as *Veleno. Una storia vera* by Giulio Einaudi editore s.p.a. in Italy in 2019. Translated from Italian by Elettra Pauletto. First published in English by Amazon Crossing in 2022.

Published by Amazon Crossing, Seattle

www.apub.com

ISBN-13: 9781542039116 (hardcover)
ISBN-10: 1542039118 (hardcover)

ISBN-13: 9781542039109 (paperback)
ISBN-10: 154203910X (paperback)

Cover design by Adil Dara

Cover image: © Rosmarie Wirz / Getty

Printed in the United States of America

First edition

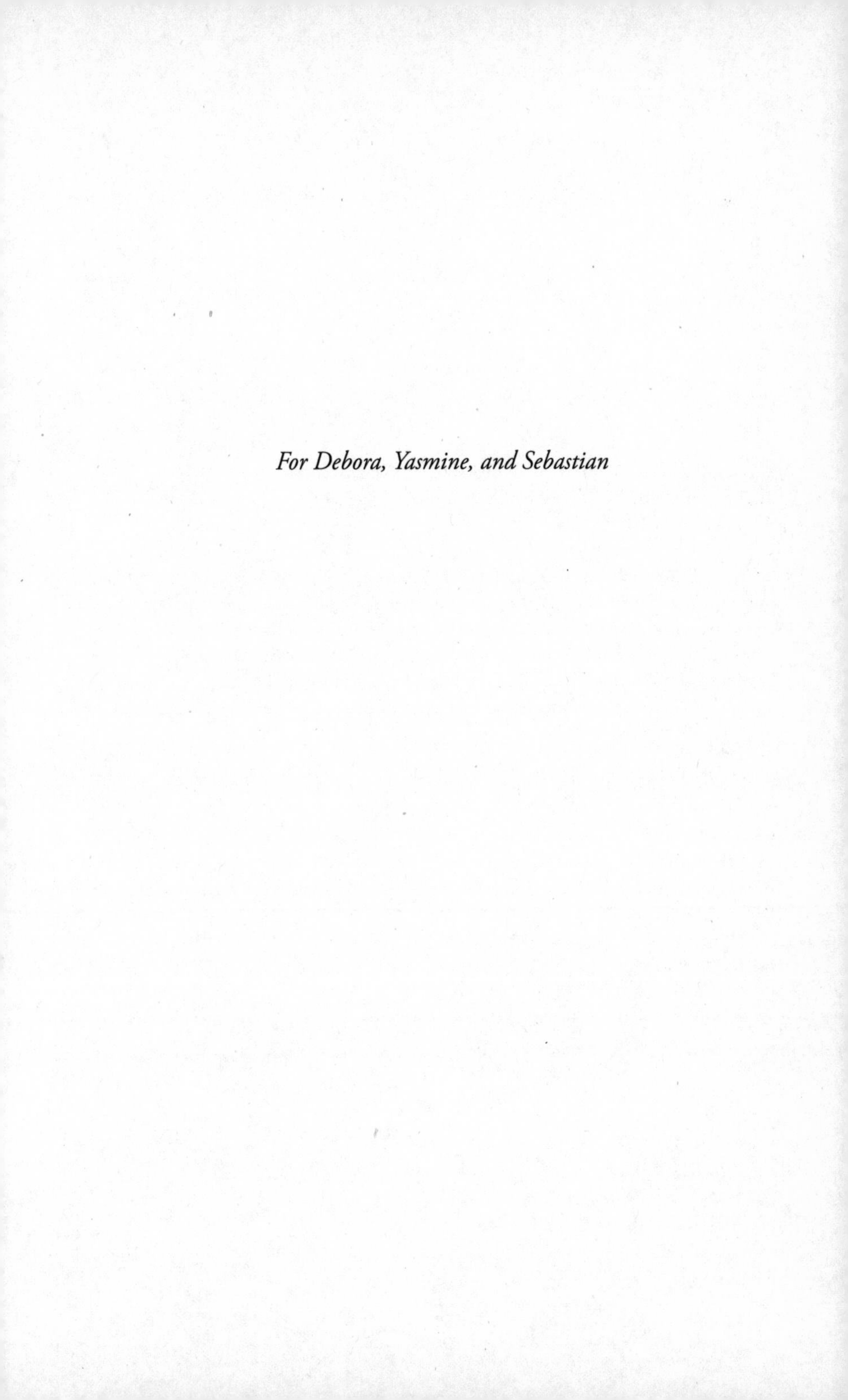

For Debora, Yasmine, and Sebastian

CONTENTS

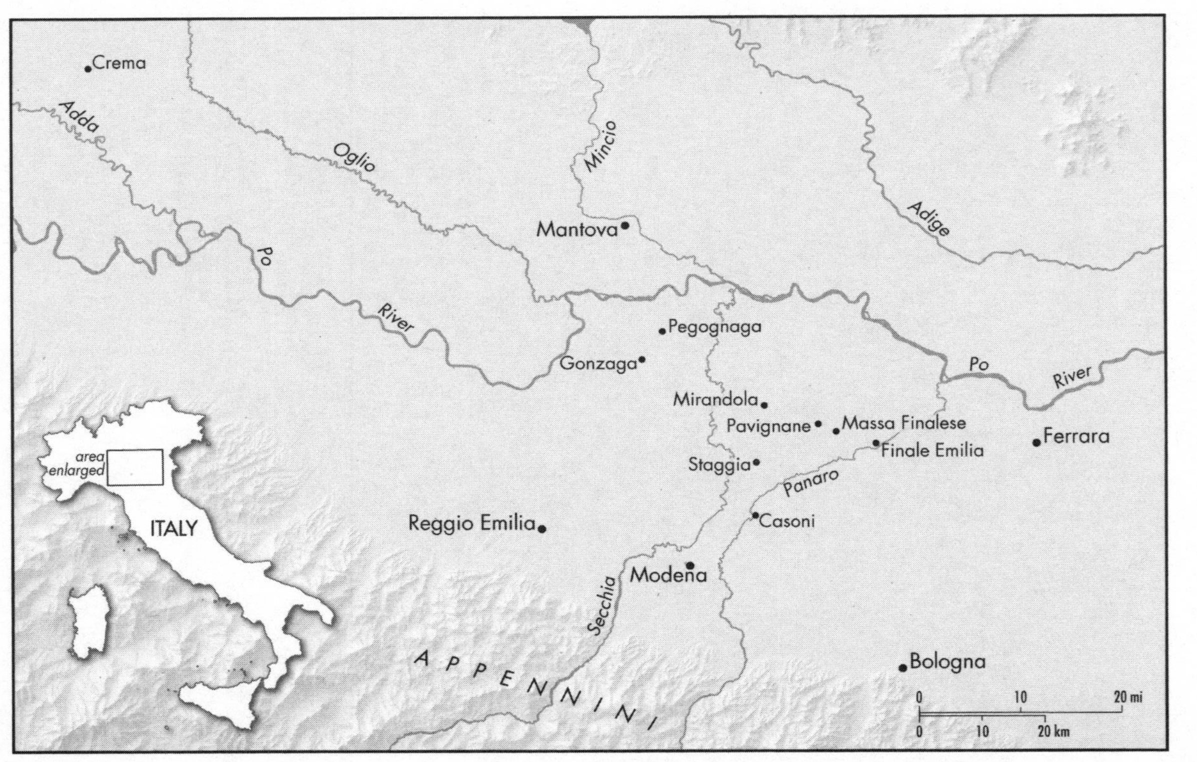
Crema
Adda
Oglio
Mincio
Mantova
Adige
Po
River
Pegognaga
Gonzaga
Po
River
Mirandola
Pavignane
Massa Finalese
Finale Emilia
Ferrara
Staggia
Panaro
Casoni
Reggio Emilia
Modena
Secchia
APPENNINI
Bologna
area enlarged
ITALY
0
10
20 mi
0
10
20 km

Finale Emilia, April 1, 1995

Five children found the skull on the riverbank. It was midafternoon on a Saturday, and five thirteen-year-olds had gone looking for a place to fish. They found a nice thicket along the left bank of the Panaro River, at the point where it bends, just outside Finale Emilia going toward Modena.

Three of them were named Andrea. The other two were named Davide and Matteo. Matteo picked up the smooth, white cranium that lay a few feet away from the water. At first, he took it for a big rock half-covered in mud.

"Oh, shit!" he yelled, dropping it on the gravel.

The boys were shocked and excited. They stuck a twig into the nasal cavity of their find and put it in a plastic bag from the Coop grocery store. They then crossed the tree-lined avenue that skirted the cemetery and rushed to bring the object to the town hall.

Along the way, they ran into two officers on patrol. "We found a skull. It was by the river," they said, breathless. The officers were skeptical. "Yeah, yeah. Today's April Fools'. Stop kidding around." But once the officers had inspected the contents of the bag, they alerted their colleagues at the state police in Mirandola and asked the five children to take them to where they'd found the skull. Officer Marco Catalani asked the boys to show him the exact location. He inspected the surrounding area but didn't find anything.

The boys, still shaken, were allowed to go home after promising to keep quiet. The police ordered lab tests and informed the deputy district attorney for Modena, Eleonora De Marco, who called Giovanni Beduschi, a professor and medical examiner and anatomical pathologist at the hospital in Modena. The lab results were on his desk soon after.

The skull was human, there was no doubt about that. But it wasn't unusual for someone to alert his institution to remains found near churches or old mass graves.

Four years earlier, in 1991, an elderly man from Campagnola Emilia had shown up at the mayor's office having found the remains of the victims of the massacre of Cavon, one of many that occurred during the Italian resistance to the Nazis. The medical examiner and his colleagues often received quite a few bone fragments, along with whatever was left of clothing and shoes.

But this case was different. What was this skull doing there *on its own*? Where were the tibias, humeri, femurs, and other skeleton pieces that are usually found nearby? Was this it? *Just this,* he was told. As if someone had cut off the head, thrown it in the river, and hidden the rest of the body elsewhere. Beduschi shrugged and moved on.

He wrote in his report that it was a morphologically small cranium. The cranial vault had crumbled with the natural contours of the bone and showed no signs of trauma—nothing that could have been caused by a firearm. The lower jaw was missing; it had detached and fallen away during the decaying process. The front teeth had met with a similar fate, and two incisors and two canines were missing. Only the cusps of the remaining teeth, sharp and solid—along with a careful examination of the cheekbones—made it possible to estimate that the subject had been young. Probably female. Probably a child.

Since the skull lacked organic material such as tissue or hair, Beduschi hypothesized a date of death fifteen years ago or more. He supposed—based on a historical rather than a biological hunch—that the skull had belonged to a young girl who'd died many years before, probably during the Second World War.

This may be why, after informing the prosecutor, Beduschi declined to pursue expensive radioactive isotope investigations or carbon dating—which were typically reserved for more recent cases or for anything of criminal consequence.

The doctor and his colleagues tried to guess the most plausible explanation for why this toothless and solitary head would be a few steps away from the river. In the end, they decided that it must have belonged to a medical student who no longer wanted it and who'd gotten rid of it in the most expedient way possible instead of returning it to the cemetery.

Beduschi took two pictures, declassified the skull and added it to the list of unidentified relics that the past, every so often, sends back to taunt the living.

The case of the Panaro River skull was opened and closed almost immediately. Beduschi didn't give it another thought. But three years later, that human bone found a few hundred feet from the cemetery would turn up again. This time, in a story of anguish, tears, and death.

PART I

CONTAGION

1.

For me, it started one morning in Monrovia, the capital of Liberia. It was October 2014, and I was there to shoot a documentary on Ebola for an Italian TV program. The epidemic had been decimating an already poor and underserved corner of West Africa. The virus had killed thousands of people in the span of a few months, despite the best efforts of local and international aid organizations to contain the spread. Signs along the road asked residents to avoid all physical contact, and the smell of euchlorine-based disinfectants filled the hot and humid air.

I was following an ambulance as it meandered between the mud and tin shacks of the poorest neighborhoods, stopping only to quickly collect bodies. Burying loved ones was strictly forbidden. The night before, a Muslim family from a beachside neighborhood had called the emergency number to report a death. When I arrived, medics were already at work. The child's body was in a bag, resting on the grass. The rain drummed on the white plastic. He'd been dead a few hours. He was only eight months old.

Neighbors had gathered under a tree to watch the medics recover the body from the bedroom. Soon after, they watched the medics load it into a pickup truck. The medics wore white hazmat suits, masks, safety goggles, and yellow gloves, and they obsessively disinfected themselves with spray. One of them approached the boy's grandfather.

"As soon as we finish," he said, "please burn the mattress where the boy slept."

The man nodded.

The little body was taken away. The mother made a desperate cry. I filmed her. Then I turned to Francesca, one of my crew members. I winked and smiled at her. "Perfect," I said. "Great shot. Lunch?"

Back in my hotel room that evening, I realized that something was wrong. I thought back to that agonizing scene and felt completely unmoved. I felt only indifference and cynicism. And not for the first time. It was as if the crying mother and the dead boy weren't real to me, just supporting characters in a movie about me. Their tragedy didn't touch me.

I continued to think about it after returning home. What had I become? I was thirty-seven years old and had somehow lost my connection to that bright-eyed twentysomething-year-old who had decided to become a journalist because he cared about people. I had to go back to being that person. I had to find a story I could dive into and let carry me away. Something to restore meaning to my life.

Then, one night when I was with my friend Luca, who's a radio program director, he called my attention to something he was reading. "Come here a sec," he said. "Look at this article." It was the story of Lorena Morselli, a kindergarten teacher in Massa Finalese, a little town outside Modena. Her life had been shattered by a lengthy trial in which she was accused of ritual satanic abuse and sexual violence against her four children, whom she hadn't seen since they were little.

Her story was chilling. At dawn on November 12, 1998, police had shown up at her door with a distancing order from Bologna's juvenile court: her eight-year-old niece had told social services that Lorena and her husband, Delfino Covezzi, were members of a cult that brought the children of Massa to local cemeteries at night in order to rape them, sell them to a band of pedophiles, and make them participate in human sacrifices. A horror story for the ages in a land where it seemed like nothing bad could ever happen.

The girl's story prompted psychologists and social workers in nearby Mirandola to ask police to rescue Lorena and Delfino's children.

Veronica (eleven), Pietro (nine), Federico (seven), and Aurora (three) were taken from their beds, and then they vanished. But Lorena was pregnant with her fifth child. To keep them from taking him, too, she fled to a small town in Provence, France, where she delivered him in hiding. That's where she was when I called her.

She spoke with a strong Bassa Modenese accent. French words dotted her speech when she became distracted: *oui, voilà, bon, donc, attendez, alors, d'accord, mais non!* Her tale wasn't always linear. It was like the flight of a butterfly, winding and uneven. At times, she would pause her story and digress to a different scene that had just popped into her head. She opened parentheticals and didn't close them. She often lost her train of thought. Then she'd give a nervous laugh and return to the point with a "well, *donc*, where were we?" When she talked about her children, she cried. Her sentences ended in choked sobs.

Her three oldest children confirmed their cousin's account, accusing Lorena of psychological violence, kidnapping, rape, and murder in cemeteries, where she and her husband forced the children to watch and actively participate in all manner of crimes.

The children were given new lives in new families. As they grew older, they came to believe that their parents should go to prison for what they'd done. Since the morning of their rescue in the fall of 1998, they hadn't wanted to have anything to do with Lorena.

Lorena and Delfino were initially sentenced to twelve years, then acquitted in December 2014 after a long judicial appeal. But Delfino never saw the end of that trial. He died of a heart attack the year before.

Lorena's fifth child, Stefano, was all she had left. For years, she gave interviews to anyone who asked. She wanted to talk about how Mirandola's social services had destroyed her life, forcing her to leave her career, her church, and her family and to hide like a criminal in a strange country. After sixteen years, she had lost everything but an unshakeable faith in Christ and a child with brown hair and blue eyes who'd kept her from going completely mad.

I didn't know whether to believe her. Her story had plenty of holes. I had questions. Why had her children said those things? I was confused, both as a journalist and as a father. Lorena said the psychologists planted stories in the children's minds, turning them against their parents. But could a psychologist really fabricate such horrible stories and convince small children to believe them? And why would they? What if Lorena really did have a dark side?

"My children weren't the only ones to be taken away," she told me. "Between 1997 and 1998, in Massa Finalese and Mirandola, social services took away fourteen . . . no, wait, fifteen . . . actually, sixteen children. All from families accused of the same things."

An enormous black hole was forming, and as Lorena reeled off names, places, verdicts, and dates with her usual clumsiness, I felt myself being drawn into it. I felt distressed, afraid, and lost like I never had before. The story was sucking me in. I had to know more. Who were the other children? What had their parents been charged with? How had Lorena's family become involved? These questions were going to help me better visualize this dusty mosaic, which had captured my attention from the get-go.

I started to gather as much material as possible on the pedophiles of the Bassa Modenese. I found some old articles online that summarized the events, but they were thin on the details. If I wanted to piece everything together, I needed documentation: verdicts, court transcripts, reports from social services and juvenile courts. Requesting access to legal documents was out of the question. Too slow. Too much bureaucracy. I started calling some of the families' defense lawyers, asking if they'd kept any files. I didn't find much. I was asking for hard copies of documents dating back years. One person had thrown them away. Another had lost them during a move. Or they'd gone missing in the earthquake that had struck the area in 2012, causing the collapse of houses and buildings. And anyway, most of the people who had worked on the case were openly suspicious of me, a journalist and an outsider. What could I possibly want, after all these years?

The impression I got from the few people who would talk to me was that for some reason, no one wanted to poke their nose into this story again. It was over. Forgotten. "Could there be some truth to the children's stories?" I kept asking. The most frequent answer was, "Maybe, but my client didn't have anything to do with it," or, "By now it's too late to establish that."

No one could remember precisely how many children had been involved or what their names were. How many adults or what their names were. How many convictions and how many acquittals. No one was fit to be my Virgil as I traveled back in time. It was hard and unpleasant work, and no one had the time for it.

To take on such a big story alone would have been too difficult, so I turned to one of my talented colleagues, a young journalist with great instincts named Alessia Rafanelli. Over the next four years, this story became our obsession.

One morning in the spring of 2015, I got in my car and drove from Milan to Massa Finalese. I didn't know anyone there. I had a few vague clues to go on but not much else. Before arriving in Massa, I stopped by the piazza in Mirandola to ask anyone who looked older than thirty-five if they remembered anything about the case or knew anyone who had been involved. Pedophiles. Rituals in cemeteries. Convictions. I was sure that in a small town like that, where everyone knows everyone, it would be easy to obtain the addresses and phone numbers ovf people who had been there. But the old men sitting on the benches outside the Caffè del Teatro furrowed their brows and looked bewildered by my questions. *Doesn't ring a bell. Are you sure this happened here? In Mirandola?* they asked. *Ahhh, yes, I do remember something. But it was a long time ago. It happened in the Bassa, though, not Mirandola!* I talked to many people who had lived there for many years, but no one seemed to remember this story. It had filled the pages of the local papers week after week, but now it was just a hazy memory of something that had happened "out there" in that land of open fields, of commuter towns where Modenesi and Mirandolesi don't like to venture, other than to find a good *osteria* every once in a while.

The amnesia seemed to extend to Massa Finalese, a village outside Finale Emilia that had also been devastated by a tidal wave of trials. I arrived from the southwest, driving through a tree-lined, two-lane street flanked by fields and a canal. Right after the welcome sign on the right, I noticed an imposing abandoned building that was three stories tall and as long as a soccer field. Farther on, an extravagant castle in neo-Gothic style from the early 1900s, complete with towers and merlons, stood out from the houses and trees. There was nothing else of note. Piazza Caduti per la Libertà, in the village center, looked more like a three-way intersection. A white marble statue stood in the middle, an unknown soldier with his left hand over his heart, his gaze on the horizon beyond the rooftops: *In remembrance of their sacrifice, Massa pays tribute to its fallen.*

It wasn't hard to identify the main meeting points of the village as they were all located within a few dozen feet of each other: the bar by the statue, run by a Chinese lady, where the kids meet for aperitifs at six p.m.; the trendy Pasticceria Ratti across the street; the Speedy, a pizza-café-snack-bar-beer-hall behind the bank, where older folks like to gather; and Bar Pesa at the eastern corner of the piazza, toward the tree-lined street that leads straight to the cemetery.

I got the same reaction I'd received in Mirandola. People narrowed their eyes, as if struggling to think back in time, but all they could remember were brief flashes of a story I seemed to know more about than they did. Everyone knew of the Covezzis, and a few people remembered that a local priest had been involved, a certain Don Giorgio, but that was about it. I couldn't believe that such a monumental story, especially in a town of only four thousand people, had ended up in the dustbin of memory. Did they really not remember? Or were they pretending not to because they didn't want to talk about it?

2.

When Romano Galliera arrived in the late 1970s, Massa Finalese was a small village bursting with opportunity. The factories near Modena were growing, and they needed laborers. The Bellentani meat processing plant at the edge of town was crawling with workers, and anyone who needed a job could always find someone willing to give them one.

Romano was short and thin, with a long face, a pronounced nose, and piercing blue eyes. His hands were wide and rough, decidedly out of proportion to the rest of his body. As a young boy, he'd had scoliosis, but it had never been treated, leaving him with a hump on his right shoulder. He was born in 1937, not far from Massa in Pilastri di Bondeno—a handful of houses surrounded by fields on the border between Emilia Romagna and Lombardy. He grew up very modestly, on a farmstead with his mother and two sisters.

He was a quiet and reserved man. He swore infrequently. He didn't drink. He smoked filterless cigarettes one after the other, though. His whole life was like one big cigarette. He smoked all of it at once, without leaving anything behind. He wasn't interested in stability or a permanent job. He never planned for or saved anything. Whatever he had, he spent immediately. Or he gambled it away on card games in the *trattorie*. And when the money ran out, he'd borrow more or he'd find some disposable job. Barring that, he'd team up with some deadbeat, slouch, or petty crook on some small, dirty job. Then he'd go back to the *trattoria*, take up his hand of cards, and start all over again. In town, they all knew him as a slacker, so they started calling him a *set etto*, a rather cruel dialect term meaning "seven hectograms." His brain was so devoid of substance it was practically dead weight. And he couldn't hold on to a job for more than a few weeks.

Romano traversed the four corners of Ferrara, Modena, Mantua, and Rovigo in search of honest jobs and unsavory ones alike. The area is known locally as the Bassa, a flat, clay-rich part of the Pianura Padana that runs from the peaks of the Reggiano Apennine Mountains to the Comacchio valleys on the Adriatic Sea. It's a plain of fields, swamps, Po River tributaries, and farms that from above looks like an immense tapestry of tens of thousands of uneven threads.

Romano noticed Adriana Ponzetto one day as he drifted through the Bassa. She was from the northern region of Friuli and had light-brown hair, big eyes, and a slightly misaligned jaw that twisted her mouth to the left. She was fifteen years younger than he was. Romano found out that Adriana and her mother liked to go to dance halls in the country, so one day, he waited outside their house and followed them at a distance as they drove to a dance hall in Cerea. Once they were inside, he tinkered with the fuses in their car. He waited for them in the parking lot, then followed them again when they left. When the Ponzetto car broke down on the side of the road, Romano was there to offer help. That is how their story began.

Igor was born in 1975. He was a skinny and quiet child who looked a lot like his mother. Two years later came Barbara, the spitting image of her father. The arrival of his children did nothing to change Romano's ways. He still worked very little and got by hand to mouth, making do with scraps he picked up along the way. The four Gallieras shared a single room in a small apartment at Number 133 on the road that connected Massa Finalese to Finale Emilia and Modena.

They were always teetering on the line that separates hardship from true hunger. More than once, Adriana had had to call on her neighbors, in secret, because she didn't even have a bag of pasta in the pantry. These same neighbors had to listen to Romano's angry outbursts against his wife when there was nothing to eat—they rang clear through the window that gave onto the courtyard.

One day, Romano caught a potential break. A local builder needed manpower to fulfill a series of contracts in Saudi Arabia and Southeast Asia. The desert was suddenly teeming with money—the oil boom of the late 1970s had created a need for roads, bridges, and the workers to build them. Romano was going to be one of them. The pay was excellent: $3,000 per month, a small fortune at the time. Hunger seemed like a distant memory when he left for Jeddah. But it was just a mirage. Romano's higher earnings didn't alleviate his family's financial woes. He was mysteriously always short on cash. Adriana would go months without receiving even 100,000 lira ($50) from Jeddah, Iran, or Pakistan.

Well-being and happiness were increasingly out of reach for Adriana. The Galliera children always looked gaunt and ragged. One time, Adriana went to a neighbor in tears after Igor—in a fit of hunger-induced anger—had opened a cupboard and smashed all her plates on the floor. One summer, they went without food, and they had no electricity because of unpaid bills. Adriana loaded the kids onto a bicycle and rode almost twenty-five miles to stay with relatives.

Adriana didn't want to ask her husband what he did with the money. She was afraid. Romano had a bad temper and was quick to violence, including with her. She knew that once he returned to Italy, any money he brought back to her would be drained in a few hours by some croupier in a Venice casino. That's where Romano went when he was earning well. But she didn't dare object too strongly. She knew she deserved better, but much as she hated the life he'd forced her into, she still loved that surly Bondenese man, just as *in buleta*—penniless—as he'd been when she married him.

By the end of the 1980s, when the bonanza in the Middle East ended, Romano had already managed to squander everything. He barely worked at all anymore. Adriana eked out a few pennies by picking pears in the fields. But the family's condition was starting to cross a line. Igor and Barbara always looked tattered. He was the gloomier, more fragile one. He was thin and pale, didn't speak much, and was very intimidated by his father. He was bullied by the kids in school, who laughed at him and beat him up, making him feel even more insecure. Barbara was more cheerful, more carefree, resilient.

Some people called them "the uglies" or "the dirties," and rumors about them started to circulate. People told mean jokes about how their mother found the money to feed them. Social services in Mirandola, the district that oversaw the whole area, sent a social worker to monitor their situation. Caritas gave them food stamps and boxes of canned goods, even though some of the townsfolk swore they'd seen Romano trying to resell cans of tomato sauce, bags of pasta, and a few steaks the butcher had given him.

Eventually, the Gallieras were evicted from their apartment at Number 133. They hadn't paid rent in four months. They moved to the second floor of a modest apartment building in the projects on Via Volta, across the street from a yellow two-story house—the home of Oddina Paltrinieri, her husband, Silvio Panzetta, and their two teenage daughters. Silvio, a large man with olive skin, knew Romano well. He'd worked with him in Saudi Arabia and had no respect for the man. He thought he was superficial and unprincipled. But Oddina felt bad for the family. A few years before, a bad car accident had destroyed her legs, leaving her in a wheelchair. But she had a strong will. She remained very active in her community and was always ready to help those in need.

She wanted to help Adriana. She gave her food and clothes, or she invited her to smoke a few cigarettes in her kitchen, where she listened to Adriana vent her frustrations. After Igor and Barbara were born, Adriana hadn't wanted any more children. When she became pregnant again, she'd had an abortion. But in late 1989, she was pregnant again. This time, she decided to keep the baby. She named him Dario.

The last member of the Galliera family was born prematurely on May 16, 1990, in Mirandola, and weighed less than 4.5 pounds. He was kept in an incubator for a few weeks before he could go home. Two years later, he was a little blond boy with blue eyes. He'd become slightly cross-eyed and had developed a few motor problems. He was always tripping and walking into things. But he was energetic and outgoing, a small joy for his two struggling parents. But he was also another mouth to feed. The family's financial woes worsened. In Igor's case, so did the psychological ones. He was still being bullied, and he was sick of it. So one day when he was fifteen years old, he threw himself into the path of an oncoming car. Miraculously, he survived, but he sustained numerous broken bones that caused him to lose his after-school job at the carpentry shop.

The Gallieras still lacked basic necessities at home. They survived thanks to help from their neighbors. Even though their apartment in the projects was rent controlled, their unpaid rent quickly piled up. Warnings from the town were becoming increasingly insistent, and on Monday, September 27, 1993, the authorities showed up with an eviction notice. The Gallieras had a few hours to gather their things and leave. As they did, movers hired by the town climbed up and down their stairs, emptying each room of its furniture. Romano couldn't take it anymore and collapsed in a corner and cried. At fifty-six years old, with a wife, three children, and the weight of repeated failure on his shoulders, he could no longer see a future. That afternoon, the family loaded a few bags into their old white Talbot. Their car would be their home now. Romano took little Dario by the hand and crossed the street to the gate of the yellow house. Oddina and Silvio had helped them so much. Romano was hoping they'd now lend him three million lira ($2,000) so he could settle his debts.

Oddina cursed him out from her doorstep. *A tse un bon da nient,* she said in dialect. "You're a good for nothing. You couldn't even pay subsidized rent in the projects. You idiot." Then she looked at Dario, a little boy of just three years, and decided that he could stay with them until the Gallieras found a place to live.

Dario walked into the yellow house in tears. His parents drove off to look for a parking lot where they could keep the car for the night. He felt lost and afraid. Oddina immediately noticed how thin he was, probably because of the Galliera diet, where the only meal of the day was a piece of bread soaked in milk. She started to earn his trust with pasta à la Bolognese and steak cut up into tiny pieces. Dario devoured the food as if he'd never seen anything like it.

Upstairs, Dario had a warm bed with clean sheets. Giulia and Claudia, Oddina and Silvio's teenage daughters, doted on him and told him bedtime stories. But Silvio was the one who loved him the most. When Dario was around, Silvio, a big, old brute of a man, shed his gruff exterior. Dario was the son he'd never had. He took advantage of the beautiful days in early fall to load him into his white RV and take him to the zoo, to the port in Livorno, and to see the planes in Pisa. Dario was happy. His parents visited him every day, and he'd even started going to daycare.

But the social services office in Mirandola caught wind of this temporary situation and sent a social worker to talk to Oddina. She suggested Oddina enter into the foster program and become Dario's legal guardian. That way, she could also collect a few hundred thousand lira (a few hundred dollars) a month. Oddina adamantly refused. She didn't need money, and she didn't want to be part of any program. The social worker insisted, but Oddina was resolute. Dario was her neighbor's son, and she would give him a bed and three warm meals a day until his family became self-sufficient enough to come and get him themselves.

That's how things had been done in the countryside since the dawn of time. That was that.

Meanwhile, the Gallieras had moved from their car and were sleeping in an apartment that belonged to the Finale Emilia church. They'd turned to a local priest, Don Giorgio Govoni, who was known for helping immigrants and the poor. He was now working on finding permanent housing for the Gallieras.

Fall turned into winter, and Christmas vacation started. The Gallieras spent Christmas day at the yellow house. They ate at the big table in the dining room, and Dario opened his presents under the tree. Dario was euphoric, but by bedtime, he'd come down with a high fever. The following morning, around nine thirty a.m., someone knocked on the door. It was a social worker from Mirandola. She was there for the boy. They'd just found him a new home in Reggio Emilia, in a center run by nuns. They were expecting him that very morning.

Oddina and Silvio begged her to leave Dario with them. He was happy, he was fitting in, and his parents could visit him every day. Why take him to live with strange nuns so far away? But the woman had a decree from Bologna's juvenile court. They had to give in. Giulia, the eldest daughter, struggled to hold back her tears as she prepared a bag for Dario.

Still slightly feverish, Dario got in the car with Giulia and Silvio. They followed the social worker's white Panda all the way to Reggio Emilia. On the way, they told Dario he'd be there for a few days, and then he'd be able to come home. But they knew it wasn't true. After more than an hour, the cars pulled up in front of a red brick building: the Cenacolo Francescano, an institute for children from poor and struggling families. A nun opened the door. Dario clung to Silvio's neck with all his might. With some effort, the nun managed to detach him and whisk him away as he wriggled and screamed. Silently, sadly, Silvio and Giulia went home.

When he found out that his son had been taken to the Cenacolo Francescano, Romano was furious. He yelled and swore and cursed the social workers. He went to Mirandola like a man possessed. He threatened everyone at the Azienda Unita Sanitaria Locale (AUSL) offices, the local health services, and chained himself to the entrance. None of it helped. All he could do was go see Dario in Reggio Emilia during visiting hours, which was difficult since he no longer had a car.

About twenty days later, Silvio, Oddina, and their daughters went to visit Dario, but he seemed off, almost indifferent to their presence. The nuns and the social workers decided that it was best if they didn't visit anymore, to avoid exposing Dario to further trauma. Social services saw him as a long-term project. He needed to live with someone able to take care of him and give him a future until he was old enough to strike out on his own. The Gallieras would be allowed to see him from time to time.

Toward the end of 1994, about one year after Dario was taken away, a young psychology intern arrived at the Cenacolo Francescano. She was twenty-six years old. Her name was Valeria Donati. One of her first tasks at AUSL was to find a family willing to foster Dario. Her first meeting with him was too brief for her to make a diagnosis, but her initial impression was that Dario was dealing with serious emotional deficiencies. Luckily, that was her field. She'd gotten her degree in developmental and educational psychology at the University of Padua before moving to Milan, where she trained in identifying mistreatment and sexual abuse against minors.

After a few months of searching, Dr. Donati found a couple that she thought could handle a difficult case like Dario's. Enrico and Nadia Tonini, of Gonzaga, near Mantua, were already raising two other foster children. Late in the spring of 1995, Dario left the Cenacolo and moved in with the Toninis. It was his fourth home in just five years of life.

Romano lost it again. He already couldn't stand the idea of his son being at the Cenacolo Francescano. And now the boy was being handed off to complete strangers. What were they doing with his son? Was someone making a profit here?

After the eviction, Romano, Adriana, Igor, and Barbara had drifted through various accommodations before Don Giorgio Govoni finally found them a permanent place to live. It was a two-story building on a dirt road in rural Massa Finalese, where they shared the bathroom and kitchen with an immigrant family from Albania. The building was old and isolated, impossible to see from the main road. The dense fog of the Bassa could quickly turn any landscape into a spectral vision. It was so thick that for most of the year, residents said it could be cut with a knife. This impoverished, damp apartment was where the Toninis brought Dario to see his parents every few weekends.

The two families did not care for each other, though the sentiment was never expressed outside their respective domestic walls. The Toninis saw the Gallieras as a highly problematic household. They believed Dario was reluctant to go there and noticed that he always returned dirty and hungry. The Gallieras thought Dario didn't like his new home at all, especially because of Matteo, one of the older children, who Dario said beat him.

Dario started first grade at the elementary school in Pegognaga in September 1996. He immediately stood out from the rest of his classmates. He was impulsive, agitated, erratic. He often turned around suddenly, without paying attention, hitting whoever was near him with his backpack. He paired sentences that had no logical connection to each other. His classmates started to give him a wide berth. He became distracted in class or interrupted lessons, forcing teachers to move him to the front row. Rita Spinardi, one of his teachers, often had to snap him to attention. They called him a little *straminato*, a Mantuan dialect term used to describe someone with their head in the clouds.

Rita was struck by Dario's eyes. His undefined expression showed no curiosity or interest in any subject whatsoever. An empty look. Dario seemed to be floating through his own little world. He was absent-minded. He always had the wrong notebook, and he couldn't keep track of his school supplies, which were always falling off his desk. Not one pencil, eraser, pencil case, or notebook escaped this fate, which regularly interrupted lessons. But despite Dario's issues with motor control and the effort needed to help him concentrate, Rita and her colleagues decided not to bring in a special needs teacher.

Then, during Christmas vacation, Mrs. Tonini noticed something strange in Dario's behavior. He seemed to struggle more than usual to concentrate on his homework. His grades were deteriorating, and he was tripping more often. He ate less than usual, and his sleep was restless. A herpes rash had developed on his mouth, probably caused by a weakened immune system.

Mrs. Tonini asked Dario's teachers to keep an eye on him. A few days after he returned to school in January 1997, one of his teachers took Mrs. Tonini aside. She'd called Dario to her desk to go over his homework, and he mentioned something that had happened during a visit with his birth family. His older brother, Igor, had scared him by "joking around under the covers" with his sister, Barbara.

Alarmed, Mrs. Tonini bombarded the boy with questions. *What was happening in the home of that poor family? What kind of tricks were they playing on each other?* But Dario wouldn't say anything, so Mrs. Tonini called Dr. Donati, the psychologist who'd recruited her to foster Dario. Dr. Donati began to see Dario up to twice a week for three months, and each time he returned from the Galliera household, Mrs. Tonini would press him for more answers.

Romano and Adriana were called to the AUSL offices and told that visits with their son would be suspended for two months. Romano did not take the news well. He threatened to douse himself in gasoline and set himself on fire. Social workers explained to him that he needed to be patient. But AUSL had started to investigate the Gallieras. They'd heard a rumor in town that Barbara was having sexual relations with other kids in front of Igor. Maybe even with Igor.

Mrs. Tonini saw that Dario's condition was worsening at a rapid pace. She'd often find him sitting quietly and looking out the window. He stuttered more. He didn't eat. He was generally fearful and was increasingly withdrawing from the world. He still wasn't concentrating on his schoolwork.

Finally, as spring came into bloom, Dario started to confide in her. On the evening of April 11, 1997, he told his foster mother that Igor had once made him lie facedown on the living room couch and had "hurt his hips." Mrs. Tonini became more alarmed than usual. Why mention this particular body part? Why the hips? Dario gave no further details. Mrs. Tonini called Dr. Donati to update her—as she always did—on each new word or expression Dario used. The weekend passed by without further incident, but on the morning of April 15, the phone at the Mirandola social services office rang again. It was Mrs. Tonini. She was sobbing. Dario had told her that his older brother had shown him his genitals. Dr. Donati's suspicions were confirmed. That pale, quiet young man was hiding a horrible secret. Igor was a dangerous pervert who couldn't contain himself, even in front of his six-year-old brother.

The next day, Dr. Donati didn't take any calls. Mrs. Tonini showed up in person, breathless, distraught, and with the news that Igor had sexually abused Dario. The boy had opened up and said his brother had forced him into oral relations, which seemed to explain the herpes on his mouth. Igor had also intimidated and threatened him. A few days later came a new, unsettling detail: Romano and Adriana had also abused him. Romano had made Dario keep his mouth shut by saying if Dario told anyone, Romano would "hurt him even more." Dr. Donati and Mrs. Tonini were starting to form a very clear picture of what had happened. On the surface, the family seemed merely poor and isolated. But, beneath the surface, they were actually a pack of monsters who were completely incapable of controlling their most base instincts.

Dr. Donati and the social workers in Mirandola immediately contacted the district attorney's office in Modena, which assigned the case to Andrea Claudiani, a thirty-one-year-old prosecutor. He listened attentively to Dario. The boy was more confident and told his story with fewer hesitations than he had during the winter, when he'd shown the first signs of distress. On May 17, a convoy of police cruisers sped through the countryside looking for Romano, Adriana, and Igor Galliera.

3.

Police cars lined up in silence to block both sides of a small road just outside Via Milazzo 15 in Mirandola. A few officers crossed the little courtyard of the red building and pressed the intercom button with the name Scotta beside it. It was four thirty a.m. on July 7, 1997. They climbed to the second floor, entered the apartment, and stood face to face with a young couple: a tall and thin twenty-two-year-old man with big ears and defined cheekbones, and a minute Thai woman with almond eyes, olive skin, and smooth black hair. The couple looked sleepy and confused. The young man asked if something had happened to his grandmother, who'd been sick for a while. Inspector Antimo Pagano, a stocky man with a long beard that highlighted his Saracen features, shook his head no. "Mr. Federico Scotta and Ms. Kaempet Lamhab?" he said. "We have a warrant to search your house."

Federico let them in, but he had questions. The men put on black, disposable latex gloves. All they would say was that he should expect an official notification. Then they turned to the apartment. They opened, lifted, and emptied everything, thoroughly. They found family photo albums in the closet, which they confiscated.

At that same time on the fourth floor of a nearby red brick building, a forty-four-year-old mother named Francesca was in tears as she watched the same scene unfolding in her own house. She was a friend of the Scottas. Police had shown up and asked her to wake her daughter, Marta, eight, and to prepare a bag for her. That's all they said. They put on their black gloves and started to go through every corner of the house. Not knowing who to turn to, Francesca had called a friend in Mirandola.

"Anna, it's Francesca," she said. "The police are here. I don't know what they want. They're taking all my pictures."

Anna didn't understand. "What pictures?"

Francesca was worried. She suspected that the search had something to do with her daughter, and she believed they were there to take her away.

"Don't worry, Francesca," Anna said before hanging up. "Everything will be OK."

Back in the Scotta home, a whimper had been heard coming from one of the bedrooms. Elisa, three, had woken up during the ruckus and had started to cry. Nick, her little brother who was just a few months old, was still sleeping. The police asked the Scottas to get the children ready. They asked for the keys to the family's Golf GT so they could search that, too. Once the sun was high in the sky, they asked that all four of them follow them to the precinct. Federico and Kaempet loaded the stroller into the trunk and climbed in. The police cruisers escorted them a few hundred feet to the police station.

Kaempet still didn't understand much Italian. The officers asked Federico to leave the kids in the waiting room for a few minutes so he could go upstairs to take care of some formalities. Elisa was left sitting in a chair; Nick was in a stroller. The Scottas were met by Marcello Burgoni, the head of Mirandola's social services. He was holding a protective order for their two children due to "serious acts of abuse." Dario, a boy from Massa Finalese, had told AUSL psychologists that Federico and his wife, Kaempet, together with the Gallieras, had abused him and their own children in various apartments in Massa and Mirandola. Federico inveighed against Dr. Burgoni and the police. He upended a table and tried to storm out of the room with his wife, but officers blocked them at the doorway. When they finally made it to the waiting room to say goodbye to their children, they found it empty. Elisa and

Nick had been taken away. Federico sat down and put his hands in his hair. Kaempet burst into tears. It was happening again.

Their story had begun in Bangkok six years before, in a pub on the other side of the world. Federico was sixteen years old and traveling with his father, a widower who regularly spent his summer vacations in Thailand. Father and son didn't get along well, so Federico spent his days alone, roaming the city and training in Muay Thai, a great passion of his. He met Kaempet in a bar in the early 1990s. She was working as a waitress. They were the same age. They started dating and soon became serious.

Once back in Italy, Federico started writing letters to her. He returned the following summer and the one after that, this time resolved never to leave her again. They got married in Thailand, and in February 1993, when they were both barely eighteen, they moved to Mirandola. Federico found shift work at a biomedical facility, while Kaempet studied Italian and got paid under the table for cleaning work. They made friends with Francesca and her daughter, Marta.

Francesca was from Casandrino, outside Naples, but she'd been living in Emilia Romagna since the mid-1970s. She raised a son there on her own, met someone new, and had a daughter with him in 1989. But their relationship ended badly. Social services had gotten involved. In the end, Francesca won custody of her daughter. The girl stayed on with her mother and grew attached to the neighbors, a young Italian-Thai couple who were expecting a child.

Kaempet had just turned nineteen when she became pregnant. Her contractions started on March 6, 1994, and she and Federico rushed to the hospital. Elisa was born that very evening. A few days later, Federico came home at nine p.m. to find the little girl crying inconsolably. Kaempet couldn't explain it. She hadn't been able to calm her.

Federico brought the little girl to Francesca for help, counting on her experience as a mother. But Elisa continued to scream until the following morning, when Federico, now very worried, decided to take her to the emergency room. Doctors immediately noticed signs of bruising, hematomas, and a fracture, as if she'd been violently beaten. Federico asked his wife for an explanation. *What happened?* Kaempet said Elisa had fallen down the stairs. But Federico didn't believe her. The doctors called the police. Finally, in tears, Kaempet told Federico that someone she knew from Thailand had hurt Elisa. According to Kaempet, the woman had tried to force her into prostitution so she could take a percentage of her earnings. When Kaempet refused, the woman retaliated by flinging Elisa against the wall. Kaempet lied about it because the woman had threatened to hurt her family in Thailand if she went to the police. Federico was furious. He screamed at his wife and threatened to leave her.

The Scottas pressed charges against the Thai woman, but the police had already alerted Mirandola's social services. As a precaution, they suspended Federico and Kaempet's custodial rights. Elisa was placed in the care of a nearby family. The Scottas would have to follow a gradual reconciliation program to get their daughter back. So they started to visit the foster family, and after a few months, they received permission to see Elisa for longer and longer periods of time. In 1997, when she was three, Elisa returned home permanently. Waiting for her there was Nick, a little brother who was just a few months old.

That summer, the Scottas, Francesca, and Marta went for a day trip to the Lidi Ferraresi to celebrate Elisa's return. They spent the day at the beach and visited the Pomposa Abbey, then they stopped at a restaurant for pizza, where they asked the waiter to take a few pictures of them. That evening, they took a walk on the beach, and Francesca and Marta hugged as they posed for a picture along the walkway. It would be their last picture together.

After the initial shock, Federico and Kaempet walked out of the waiting room where they'd seen their children for the last time. They heard someone calling their names. It was Francesca. She was sobbing. The police had forced her to follow them there with Marta. Francesca had held her daughter tight, refusing to let go, but in the end, social services had prevailed. Her daughter had also been taken away. Dario, the little boy from Massa Finalese who'd accused the Scottas, had also named Francesca and Marta. Francesca was inconsolable. "If they don't bring her back to me, they'll have to carry me out in a coffin," she kept saying.

The three of them sat down in protest, taking up the narrow sidewalk in front of the police station. Officers kept making them leave, and they kept coming back. Francesca had some razor blades with her, and when the police tried to escort her away, she used them to cut her arms. She and the Scottas stood there proclaiming their innocence as a small crowd of onlookers started to gather. A few local journalists took notes for stories. Francesca and the Scottas spent all of July going back and forth between the police station, social services, and the juvenile court in Bologna, like three pathetic pilgrims. No one would listen to them or see them. Not even the Cuirassier guards at the Quirinal Palace, where they showed up on August 1 to demand a meeting with President Scalfaro.

Francesca was sliding deeper into depression. She and Marta were extremely close, and before Marta was taken, they were almost always together. When she and Marta's father separated, Francesca had clashed repeatedly with the social workers on the case. She couldn't handle the fact that these women were speaking to her daughter, that they wanted her to see a psychologist, that they insisted she see her father. Only a few months before her removal, AUSL had written a report on Marta that described her as well cared for and very close to her mother and said that if Francesca was guilty of anything, it was of being a bit too anxious about her daughter. Francesca found Marta's absence intolerable. She felt completely alone and abandoned, even by her closest friends. Anna, whom she'd called the morning the police had come, wanted nothing to do with this story. She also had a young daughter and didn't want to risk attracting attention. Fear led many people in Francesca's life to disappear from one day to the next.

Francesca and Kaempet prepared a few boxes of clothes and toys for the kids, but the social workers were strict and told them they would pass on no packages, no presents, and no messages. Meanwhile, papers across the country were reporting instances of sexual abuse on a daily basis. In Torre Annunziata, near Naples, seventeen people had been arrested for abusing twenty students at an elementary school. In nearby Caserta, there was a ten million lira ($5,000) bounty on a pedophile who was approaching children outside a school. A bar owner in Florence had been arrested for throwing drug parties with minors, while in Monza, near Milan, five people had abused three sisters in their mother's store. In Milan, a sixty-eight-year-old man had been accused of abusing six children between the ages of nine and eleven, and a rehab counselor was indicted for committing sexual acts on minors under the age of fourteen. And now, in the province of Modena, one of the biggest cases in history was about to blow up.

Toward the end of August, Francesca and the Scottas were finally summoned to the court in Bologna to pick up their court files. Someone had accidentally left the children's new addresses on yellow Post-it Notes. Federico found out that his children had been placed in different homes. Elisa had returned to the family that had looked after her until she was three. Nick was sent farther away, to a different town outside Modena. "Federico, I read that Marta is at the Cenacolo Francescano in Reggio Emilia," Francesca whispered to him after they left. "Will you come with me?"

When they got to the Cenacolo, the courtyard was empty, and the big wooden gate was locked. On the façade above the gate was a red emblem of Saint Francis between two wolves. *Fiat pax in virtute tua et abundantia de manibus tuis,* it read. Kaempet stayed in the car while Federico and Francesca walked around the building. They heard children's voices and saw that the east side opened onto a tree-lined courtyard surrounded by green netting. Francesca stopped to peer through the gaps. She jumped back when she saw her daughter standing under the pine trees, just a few feet away. She called her name two or three times. Marta turned around and ran over to her.

"Mommy didn't forget about you!" said Francesca, fighting back tears. She threw Marta's stuffed animal, the one she liked to sleep with, over the fence. Marta asked if she'd come to pick her up. No, it wasn't possible yet, Francesca told her. Besides, Sister Annarita Ferrari, an energetic woman in her fifties, had seen them. She made Marta go back inside. She then turned on Francesca. How had they found her? Who'd given her permission to come? Who was that man with her? Under no circumstances could they be there. They had to leave right away.

On the way home, Francesca felt relieved. It had been hard for her to see Marta through that thick netting, but at least she'd made contact. Two days later, the police arrived with an arrest warrant for her and Federico for "tampering with evidence." They were taken to Modena's Sant' Anna jail and kept there for a week until the judge granted them house arrest.

On September 23, 1997, social workers took Elisa and Marta to Milan to see gynecologist Cristina Maggioni and her colleague, Maurizio Bruni. Dr. Maggioni found it striking that the shy little girl with brown hair submitted to the exam without batting an eye. She was uncommonly acquiescent for an eight-year-old. She didn't resist, and she was completely unperturbed. When they touched her to determine if she had any lesions, she seemed to be "elsewhere," almost "dissociated." Dr. Maggioni believed this was typical among children who'd suffered extreme abuse. In her experience as a technical consultant for the Milan district attorney's office, she'd seen many such cases. The exam later confirmed her initial suspicions. The seriousness of the abuse exceeded anything she'd ever seen. But it wasn't possible to establish the time frame of the abuse with certainty. It could have started many years before and continued over time. Or it could have taken place up to four years before. After the exam, Dr. Maggioni approached Marta and told her that there were "signs" down there. Then she looked her in the eye and told her not to keep any secrets. If she had something to say, she should say it.

The exam results were soon leaked to the press. Francesca and Federico learned about them by chance two days later while watching the Televideo news. They heard about the "numerous, mutually congruent marks that made it highly likely that she'd been abused," and the serious damage she had sustained that could compromise any future pregnancies. Dr. Maggioni said she'd never seen anything so horrific in twenty years on the job.

Francesca was alone in her apartment and on house arrest. She couldn't call anyone other than her lawyer. She fell into a deep depression and didn't come out of it. A little boy had accused her of participating in parties where children were being forced into sex acts in exchange for money, and now a medical exam seemed to confirm it.

Around lunchtime on Sunday, September 28, Francesca called her lawyer, Ettore Savoca, crying. He tried to comfort her, reminding her of a hearing due to take place the following week at the court of liberty (now the court of reexamination). "I don't care about liberty," she said. "I just care about my little girl."

At two p.m., the Scottas' phone rang. Federico, also on house arrest, couldn't answer. Kaempet picked up and put the phone on loudspeaker. Francesca was ranting. She seemed drunk.

"I love you. I can't do this anymore. Try to stay calm and defend yourselves however you can."

Federico tried to say something, but she'd already hung up. Fearing the worst, they called the police. Francesca wrote a note. *I'm innocent. I just want my little girl back.*

When Mirandola patrolman Antonio Presti arrived at the red brick building at Via Statale 12, he saw someone leaning over the balcony on the fifth floor. He and his partner ran inside and up the stairs. The door was held closed by a chain, but they managed to open it just enough to see Francesca straddling the railing. Presti and his colleague kicked down the door, but Francesca was already in the air. She was declared dead at the ER in Mirandola a few hours later.

The next day, Marta didn't go to school. The sisters at the Cenacolo told her someone important was coming to see her. Marta hadn't seen her mother in a month. At first, she missed her and asked to go home. She continued, when questioned, to say that nothing had happened to her there. But as the weeks went by, her feelings started to become confused and contradictory. Since being taken away, she'd been under the care of AUSL psychologist Valeria Donati. She told Dr. Donati and Sister Annarita that she was a little scared to see her mother again. Especially after the medical exam: Dr. Maggioni had told her plainly that there was a problem "down there," so something must have happened. Marta had to try to remember what it was, she was told, because sometimes people forget bad things that happen to them. Marta was confused; she really couldn't remember anything. Yet Sister Annarita continued to insist Marta tell her what happened.

One Monday morning, something changed. No one came to ask her questions about her mother. Dr. Donati arrived at the Cenacolo with a social worker and took her aside with Sister Annarita. When they told her that her mother was gone, Marta leaned forward and rested her head on the nun's knees. She cried until she fell asleep. When she woke up, she went to play with the other children. In the following days, she repeatedly asked when she could see her mom again.

"She's dead," Sister Annarita kept telling her. "If she did something wrong and repented, then she's with the Lord."

After that, Sister Annarita often saw Marta praying at her bedside. "I hope Mommy repents. That way she'll go to Jesus."

"Why?" asked the nun. "What do you think she did?"

"She hit me when I was bad."

Marta had a hard time that fall. Weeks of conflicting memories and feelings were piling up. The nuns noticed that the girl's neck was "swollen," which they thought was a psychosomatic reaction to her distress. She wasn't eating, she wasn't playing, she wasn't paying attention in class, she wasn't sleeping well, and when she did, she had nightmares.

She swung back and forth between the certainty that nothing bad had ever happened to her and the doubt that in some remote corner of her memory, there was a box she wasn't brave enough to open. A box that contained something bad. And the women who were now taking care of her with so much love were asking her to unburden herself of it. One evening in December, before bedtime, Marta told one of the sisters of the Cenacolo that she was afraid of the dark. She was afraid someone was going to take her away.

"Who's going to take you away?" asked the sister.

"The people who are hurting me."

"What people?"

"I'm scared. I'm ashamed."

She started to build up her courage. She opened the box she'd been avoiding for more than five months and looked inside. Her mother,

Francesca, had decided to throw herself off a balcony to avoid facing the truth. She'd left Marta alone in the world with her sadness and guilt. No, her mother hadn't been so good to her, after all. Sometimes she took her to an apartment outside Mirandola. To the home of two men named Marco and Matteo. They abused her. They took pictures or videos of her, and when they were done, they gave money to her mother. Sometimes her mother's friend, Federico Scotta, would be there. She'd also seen other children in that apartment. Marta tried hard to remember their names, or where the apartment was, but it was really hard. Something was blocking her. Maybe it was trauma. Maybe it was shame. Maybe it was fear.

"Do you know a boy named Dario?" asked Dr. Donati. "He's the one who mentioned you." But Marta couldn't remember. She was confused and uncomfortable.

One day, the children were watching a cartoon on TV with a teacher. Some skulls appeared on screen. Marta seemed to perk up and recover a fragment of memory. Her mom had a skull, too. She'd also seen some at Marco and Matteo's house. Dr. Donati and Dr. Burgoni became alarmed. A year had passed since Dario had shown the first signs of distress. Maybe his long silences, insecurities, and hesitations—the signs that had sparked Dr. Donati's initial suspicions—were actually hiding a much darker secret. Maybe the people the children had named in Massa Finalese and Mirandola weren't just a band of pedophiles, content with buying and selling children for a few hundred thousand lira. Maybe that was just the beginning. Maybe there was more. And given what they'd seen so far, it was sure to be something ugly.

4.

The two men arrived one cold day in January. Dario saw them approach Vittorino da Feltre Elementary School in Pegognaga during recess. One of them, the thin one, had a black mustache and ocher-colored hair—probably a wig. The other, the fat one, had curly hair and glasses, and he wore weird short boots with a sort of heel. They were an unsettling pair, and they were both named Giorgio. With a quick step, Giorgio and Giorgio slipped unnoticed through the old, gray gate that enclosed the red school building. They quickly crossed the courtyard, ducked under the building's arches, and in an instant, they were in the hallway. Dario recognized them immediately. He was petrified. The men asked him to follow them. Dario obeyed without a peep. Nobody noticed as the three of them reached the gate and headed toward a nearby gym. A dark-blue car was waiting for them there. Dario felt scared and intimidated and didn't speak. But he remembered one thing: there was a flashing yellow light on the roof of the car. When he saw the driver, he shuddered. He'd seen him recently in a cemetery and was very afraid of him. The man had white hair and was wearing a black shirt, black pants, and a black see-through cap with some kind of a crest on it. The two Giorgios pushed Dario into the car, then they took off for Massa Finalese. After about forty minutes, the group stopped at a very big restaurant. It was all pink, and the parking lot was covered in pebbles. Dario didn't want to go in, but one of the men pushed him, causing him to fall. The walls of the restaurant were covered in big, dark mirrors and the curtains were white. The place was empty, but the waiter—who introduced himself as Franco—seated the men, who ate alone, without offering anything to Dario. When they were done, they all climbed back into the car and drove down a long, tree-lined street before stopping in front of the cemetery.

Giorgio and Giorgio dragged Dario to two tombstones that were side by side.

"See these?" they asked him in a threatening tone. "That's where we're going to bury your new parents."

The message was clear: Dario had already said too much to his psychologists and to the district attorney. From now on, he would have to keep his mouth shut. Then they drove him back to school and left him out front, just before the bell rang and the courtyard filled with moms.

Dario didn't know what to do. It wasn't the first time the men had threatened him. It had happened once before, around Christmas. His biological mother, Adriana, was with them that time. Dario saw her from the school gate, looking at him sternly. She called out to him without getting out of the car. "Dario!" she said. "Your father is suffering!" One of the men went up to the gate, grabbed him by the arm, and ordered him to leave with them. But Dario managed to get away with the help of two classmates.

Dario had managed to keep that event to himself for all of winter break. He hadn't even told Mrs. Tonini. But the two men made clear that they could do whatever they wanted, whenever they wanted to. If he reported them, what would happen to his foster parents? Would they hurt them, too? Would he be forced to change houses again?

When Mrs. Tonini came to pick Dario up at four fifteen p.m., she found him agitated and shaken.

"What happened?" she asked. With a trembling voice, Dario told her about the blue car outside the school, about his mother and the two Giorgios. She decided not to do anything. She left him alone until the next day. Then she asked again, "What happened?"

Dario told her everything, including what happened at the restaurant and the cemetery. Mrs. Tonini called the school in Pegognaga. She knew the teachers and staff well—her two older foster children had also gone there. Rita answered. Mrs. Tonini asked if the gates stayed locked during school hours. Rita said no, they usually remained open. Mrs. Tonini told her about the strange visit from two men who twice had threatened her son and on one occasion had even taken him out of school. Could they at least prevent access to the building after the children had entered? "Certainly," Rita assured her.

But nothing would calm Dario down. He was in the throes of terror, which forced him back into himself. Mrs. Tonini didn't know how to comfort the poor boy. He'd been with her for three years and had become her son in every sense of the word after he was taken from the Gallieras for good. She was a wreck, as she'd told Dr. Donati many times. She knew she had to listen to Dario's stories, but they tormented her and made her feel incredibly anxious, powerless, and insecure. They were reminders of her inability to truly help him.

A year had passed since Dario had spoken of his older brother fooling around under the covers, eleven months since he had seen his parents for the last time, and eight months since the *carabinieri* had surrounded the Galliera house in Massa Finalese and arrested Dario's parents and brother. When the *carabinieri* took them away on May 17, 1997, they were all crying. Officers searched the house, finding and seizing some pornographic magazines. Not long after, Igor made a partial admission, revealing a morbid and perverse nature. Dario wasn't lying, not completely, he said. They had, in fact, touched each other's private parts. But then he immediately tried to pin the blame on his little brother, saying Dario was the one who'd asked him to do it. But that was as far as it went. Sure, he'd also gotten handsy with his sister, Barbara, but he'd stopped right away, because his mother had scolded him. As for abuses by his father, Igor said he didn't know anything. The only thing he could remember was that one night, he'd heard Dario whine and ask his father to let him sleep.

Romano and Adriana Galliera denied the accusations, but Igor's words landed them in serious trouble. In the spring of 1997, Dario seemed to have found the courage to reveal other incidents that had occurred outside the Galliera home. These involved other children as well. Mrs. Tonini continued to take diligent notes of everything Dario said, passing the information on to Dr. Donati, who delved deeper and gathered additional details during her sessions with him. Sometimes, Dario said, Romano would take him to a neighbor's house, where two people would be waiting for him. The woman's name was Rosa, and the man went by "Ales." Dario clearly remembered the words his father exchanged with this woman on at least one occasion. *I'll leave you the boy if you give me some money,* Romano said before he left.

Rosa was a strange woman who liked strange things. She promised Dario that if he did what she said, she'd keep him with her and let him do whatever he wanted. He wouldn't even have to go to school anymore. She lived in a house in the country far from prying eyes. When Dario was there with her, she made him hit her with a fire poker and perform sex acts while her husband "Ales" took pictures with a Polaroid camera. Dario couldn't remember anything else. Those things had happened when he was little and still living with his parents, so likely when he was about three years old. But there was one detail Dario had never forgotten. When his father came to pick him up, the couple would give him money for his service. Dr. Donati watched Dario's body language as he talked. He looked miserable. That couple must have really traumatized him.

After finishing his story, Dario walked up to the window and opened it. He said he wanted to throw himself out of it. He said he wanted to die. Then he sat on Dr. Donati's lap and curled up into a ball.

His father may have been sick in the head, so wicked as to sell his little boy to his friends, but why didn't his mother protect him? Dario had an explanation. Adriana and Barbara also went to that wretched house. They also liked to be beaten with fire pokers.

Mrs. Tonini was furious. Before these revelations, she'd felt a mixture of pity and disgust for that gaunt, ignorant woman who couldn't even feed and clothe her son. Now, she was overcome with so much anger that she could no longer hide it from Dario. How could his mother allow such a thing? Was she so afraid of Romano that she'd go along with anything?

Dario listened and nodded. He was angry now, too. But he was still holding on to some guilt, a common experience for victims of sexual abuse, even though they are not at fault. Who were those friends of his parents? Where did they live? Dario strained to piece together his memories and give them shape. They must be from around Massa Finalese, but he couldn't say for sure where that "old but big house" was located. Mrs. Rosa was married and didn't have kids. He couldn't remember what she looked like. She might have had brown hair. Ales, the husband who took the Polaroids, looked like his new grandfather, Mr. Tonini's father, "a big man, with a mustache."

The police looked into it. One of Romano Galliera's known associates was a fat, fifty-year-old man with tattoos, dark hair, and a big, black mustache. He was from Massa Finalese, but his name wasn't Ales, it was Alfredo, and he was known around town as "Alfredone" or "Fredone." He had a terrible reputation and a long rap sheet for crimes including extortion and dealing in stolen goods. He didn't have a steady job, he often played cards, and he didn't hesitate to use his big, fat hands to lob a couple of *sciafòn* upon the face of some unlucky chump. The townsfolk also said he was a pimp and had one or two girls working for him. Galliera was thought to be one of his gofers. Fredone made him run errands and do various odd jobs.

At that time, Fredone lived in a country house in Scortichino, less than fifteen minutes from Massa. A certain Rosa Maria also lived there. When inspector Antimo Pagano from the Mirandola police went to arrest them, Rosa seemed genuinely shocked. Fredone a little less so. He was used to the police, searches, nights in jail. "Let's hope Romano didn't fuck something up," Inspector Pagano heard him say. He was referring to Romano's problems with his youngest son and subsequent arrest. But Rosa was extremely agitated and kept asking the police what they wanted. Fredone started to laugh.

"Don't worry, we'll be home by morning."

Rosa learned of her charges at the jailhouse in Ferrara. She and her husband, acting in concert with other suspects, had allegedly violated several newly ratified articles in the penal code governing norms against sexual violence. Once in her cell, Rosa collapsed to the ground. She hadn't even been allowed to bring a change of clothes. When he heard the charges, Fredone, detained in Modena, stopped laughing.

A week later, prosecutors showed Dario pictures of their suspects. He pointed to the picture of a man, then backtracked. Ales's face wasn't among them. But soon after leaving the office with Mrs. Tonini, he asked to go back. He pointed to the picture of a big, fat man holding a boy. It was Fredone.

Dario gathered the courage to reveal everything. After months of silence, Dr. Donati had finally helped him understand that he didn't have to be afraid anymore. He was safe now. Yes, it would be hard to talk about it, but he'd feel a lot better if he could lift that weight off his shoulders. So, he pulled out more names. "Lady R. and her dealer," as some of the local papers called them, weren't his only abusers. His parents had also taken him to the apartment of two guys who drove around on Vespas, a red one and a black one. He'd seen other children there, too. Their parents would leave them there for a few hours. He witnessed abuses of all kinds, but he couldn't identify the place or these two tormenters.

Francesca and Federico's names were plucked from a long list of suspects. And the names of two little girls from Mirandola, Elisa and Marta, popped up among the list of victims. Dr. Donati was seeing these two little girls already, Elisa because of a violent injury, and Marta because of a difficult parental separation. They were neighbors, and their parents, Francesca and Federico, were friends. Even though they lived ten miles outside Massa, Dario knew them both.

5.

By the summer of 1997, only three months after Dario's first revelations, the pedophile network had already reached a ten-mile radius, encompassing Massa, Bondeno, and Mirandola. On July 11, as radio stations played Puff Daddy's latest hit, "I'll Be Missing You," on repeat, Dario, Dr. Donati, and one of her colleagues were at social services meeting with Alberto Ziroldi, the Modena judge for preliminary investigations. With some effort, Dario managed to tell him about the abuses.

A few days later, indictments were sent out for Romano, Adriana, Igor, Rosa, Fredone, the Scottas, and Francesca. Francesca committed suicide that September, so the other seven defendants would go to trial without her. For Modena's prosecutors, everything seemed ready. They had Dario's testimony. They had the results of Elisa's and Marta's medical exams and believed that Marta would talk sooner or later. It seemed obvious to them that the defendants had their backs against the wall.

Around that time, Dr. Donati went to see prosecutor Andrea Claudiani. She was alarmed and needed to talk to him urgently. Dario, back from summer vacation in Gargano with the Toninis, had mentioned some new and even more sinister events. Claudiani stopped what he was doing and listened.

Dario had remembered another name: Giorgio. Romano knew him and had taken Dario to his house. He was a mayor, Dario thought, but he wasn't sure. In fact, he immediately corrected himself. Maybe he was a doctor. But maybe not. Dario was confused. He'd actually met two men named Giorgio. The first one was the one Romano knew, who raped him and Marta in exchange for money. The second one was married to a woman who wore her black hair in braids. Dr. Donati and Mrs. Tonini focused on the first one, the mayor who might be a doctor. They called him "Giorgio One." Mrs. Tonini suggested that Dario's description sounded more like a priest. She was right.

Nothing and no one terrified Dario more than this man and his homonymous partner, "Giorgio Two." They'd told him he'd burn in hell, and since then, he'd had terrible nightmares. *Hell.* That word opened a floodgate of bad memories from the last time he'd seen his birth parents before he was taken away for good. Meanwhile, the word set off alarm bells for Dr. Donati and reminded her of an incident Dario had casually mentioned a while back. When he was little, he'd been to someone's funeral, maybe that of a relative. He saw a woman carrying a coffin, and this had made an impression on him. Could these two events be connected? The funeral and the two Giorgios who threatened hell? Yes, Dario answered. They were connected.

A cemetery at night. "Giorgio the mayor" in a tunic. Some adults standing around him. Romano, Adriana, Igor, Barbara, Federico, Francesca, Rosa, and Ales the photographer. Some of them wore tiger, panther, or vampire masks. They were performing a ritual of some kind. They opened a few coffins and locked the children inside. Dario, Elisa, and Marta were each laid in a coffin with a cross on top. It was dark inside, and Dario couldn't get out because the lid was too heavy. He tried to push, but his little arms were too weak to dislodge the wood-and-metal slab. He remembered crying and hearing the grown-ups laughing. Then someone took the lid off, and the shapes reappeared around him as his lungs filled with the cold night air. "Mayor Giorgio" announced in a serious tone that they'd been transformed into the children of the Devil. Then he ordered the adults to cudgel them.

But was he really a mayor? Or a doctor? If he was wearing a white tunic and performing a ritual, maybe he was something else. Dario added details about him as he recounted his story. He was about 1.7

meters (5.5 feet), chubby, with dark, curly gray hair and glasses. He wore men's shoes with a heel. During the ritual, he gave Dario a knife and told him to kill a black cat. Dario hit it weakly, wounding it. Igor dealt the death blow. Ales laughed and ripped off one of the animal's limbs and held it to his face, as if he was going to eat it. This was the part of the story that troubled Dario the most. He loved animals, especially the Tonini family cat. He hated the thought of having hurt animals sacrificed during the rituals, including a dog. Sometimes Dario cried inconsolably during his sessions with Dr. Donati. God only knows what other horrors he'd witnessed among the tombstones of that cemetery. Dario couldn't remember where it was, but, and of this he was sure, there was a church.

After Dario first mentioned the Giorgios, Mirandola's police inspector Antimo Pagano started to investigate. He consulted police archives and visited towns around the Bassa. He started with the Massa Finalese cemetery. It was on the northern tip of town, along Via Albero, a two-lane road that cuts through fields and changes to Via Imperiale before it crosses Burana Canal a few miles from the Lombardy border.

Pagano noted that the cemetery had a "more or less rectangular shape" and was surrounded by a wall. The cast-iron gate at the entrance was closed, but there was a second entrance on the southern end. It was newer and gave out onto a parking lot. The main path led to a church similar to the one Dario had mentioned. It contained one large room with a small altar. A modest chandelier was hanging overhead. Pagano noticed an opening along the left side, where the gravedigger's equipment was stored. It led to a series of interconnected rooms—the charnel house. Inside were an old wooden coffin with a crucifix on its lid and a few caskets. The longest one was three feet at most. Pagano spoke to the people who lived in the homes nearby, but no one had ever seen anything odd. Someone in town told him he'd heard about a group of cyclists that had noticed unusual movements in the cemetery one late afternoon, but Pagano couldn't track them down.

Dario said that the Giorgio who ran the rituals lived near a bell tower. So, Pagano started to look into every Giorgio in the province who had something to do with churches or cemeteries. He found two. One worked as a gravedigger at the cemetery in Concordia, not far from Mirandola. The other was Don Giorgio Govoni, the vicar of Staggia and San Biagio, which placed him right in the "zone of interest." Pagano was shocked when he read those names. He wasn't from the area—he'd moved to Mirandola from Naples for work—but he knew these places. While off duty, he'd gone to town fairs there or to see live nativity scenes. He remembered the vicar of those little country churches—he looked a lot like the man Dario described. He had curly hair, he was overweight, and he wore glasses. Pagano also remembered another detail. During a town fair, he'd glimpsed a pair of boots, the kind people used to wear a long time ago, under the priest's vestments. He returned to investigate in plain clothes one Sunday after the last morning Mass. Don Giorgio and his congregation were gone, aside from three women who'd stayed behind to pray. Pagano noticed that the Staggia and San Biagio churches both had bell towers. And the sacristy in San Biagio seemed to match Dario's description as it was connected to the cemetery by a path lined with cypress trees. Pagano found the schedule of funerals from the year before and noticed that some of the burials and exhumations to dispose of old bodies had taken place right around the time Dario was visiting his birth family. Pagano looked around. Don Giorgio's church was surrounded by a few houses and a barn. Pagano was tempted to go knocking and see who lived there. He had questions. But instinct held him back. The priest was well known and beloved in the area. He would be alerted immediately if someone came asking questions about him or about what happened in the cemeteries. Best to keep a low profile and continue to investigate from behind the scenes.

Don Giorgio Govoni was an institution in the Bassa Modenese. Even the social workers knew him. He'd been helping the Galliera family for some time, including by finding them that home in the country after their last eviction. After they lost their car, he helped them run errands, and he even drove Igor to meet his lawyer in Modena. The kid couldn't even find a simple address on his own—Modena was a much bigger place than the one in which he'd grown up. Initially, Dario said he didn't know Don Giorgio. But then he changed his mind. Giorgio One, the mayor in the tunic, the sadistic rapist at the helm of the band of pedophiles, was none other than Don Giorgio Govoni. It had to be him. The monster. Everything made sense to the investigators. That's why the priest was so kind to those dunces, who didn't even deserve welfare assistance, who didn't even go to church, and who resold donated food in order to buy cigarettes while their children roamed the streets in rags. Something in that family must have caught his eye: a little boy. Don Giorgio's circuitous moves amounted to child grooming—a tactic commonly used by sexual predators that involves making friends with parents and relatives before targeting a young victim. It creates the ideal conditions to act without interruption. In this case, the priest seemed to have pressed the entire Galliera family into becoming financially and psychologically dependent on him—all to get to that confused little boy. The headlines were all over it: "Sex party with kids, there was even a priest." "A boy accuses a priest 'he knew'; Don G." "The meetings were filmed, on 'set' with sacred relics."

At his table at the Trattoria dalla Marta—a popular stop for truckers, farmers, and workers from rural San Felice sul Panaro, near Massa Finalese—Don Giorgio Govoni didn't seem too worried about the charges. Even though the press hadn't named him directly, they'd dropped some pretty obvious clues as to his identity. Everyone knew it was him, and as folks from the surrounding towns and parishes read the leaks filtering out daily from the district attorney's office in Modena, they started to voice doubts about his character. The priest put on a brave face—or tried to—for his closest friends. It was all a big misunderstanding, he said with a shrug. The truth would come out sooner or later. He was too distinguished, too respected, too beloved for people to take those hateful insinuations seriously. In more than a half century, he'd never had a problem with the law, or with the thousands of parishioners in San Felice, Finale Emilia, Massa, Camposanto, Staggia, or San Biagio. Since the middle of the 1960s, he'd been baptizing, confirming, marrying, and burying them. It was hard to find a parish or oratory in the area that he hadn't graced with a Mass, an organized trip, or a skating rink for the kids. But these weren't the main reasons why people liked him above other priests. This was the heart of Emilia Rossa, Red Emilia, a land of hard work and even harder workers, and Don Giorgio was a man of the people. He didn't just stand behind an altar reciting sermons and blessing souls. He rose at the crack of dawn, climbed into his truck, and earned his living grinding away the miles until nighttime, just like everyone else. The trucker-priest, that's what they all called him.

Don Giorgio was born in 1941 in Dodici Morelli, a village near Finale Emilia. He was the second of three boys born to a trucker. From the start, he seemed destined to the priesthood. After the Second World War, when he was six years old, an uncle took him on a pilgrimage to San Giovanni Rotondo. When they returned, the uncle told everyone that Padre Pio of Pietrelcina, walking through the crowd, had suddenly stopped in front of Giorgio, a little boy with dark, curly hair and small eyes, laid his bandaged hand on his forehead, and said, "You will become a priest." The Saint had been right. After fifth grade, Giorgio told his mother he wanted to be ordained. He joined an ancient seminary in Nonantola, near Modena. It was a hard choice, but a brave one.

He faced frigid winters and six-month periods away from his family. Only a strong faith could survive that.

He received his cassock five years later, and in 1966 he became a fully fledged priest. At the same time, Giorgio had also gotten his tractor-trailer license. He wanted to continue his father's work after he'd died young. When he wasn't celebrating Mass, Don Giorgio loaded and off-loaded beets and wheat for the new Emilian co-ops. He loaded and off-loaded piles of dirt that arrived in Mirandola and Sassuolo from Germany to supply the ceramic industry that was turning this region of artisans into a powerhouse of the Italian economy. Then he clocked out and became a priest again. With a Toscanello dangling from his lips, he spread the Gospel, resolved disputes, and worked late into the night to organize church fairs and pilgrimages. He was in constant motion, stopping only to gulp down a plate of minestrone and a glass of wine at the nearest country tavern, especially the Trattoria dalla Marta, which had become his base since he'd moved to San Felice sul Panaro in the mid-1980s.

During that time, newcomers from the first wave of African migrations started to pour into the countryside around the Bassa. More would arrive in the following years. Soon, these groups of *maruchín* and *nègar*, as some locals called them, were moving into dilapidated buildings that had been abandoned since the start of the century. During the day, they would go around offering their services to local farmers and businesses, and at night, they would drag their plastic bags across dark fields to return home to country hovels with no gas or electricity. The trucker-priest started to track down the owners of these abandoned buildings. He wanted to have the houses renovated in exchange for the permission to shelter these struggling, hungry people who were becoming a growing source of labor.

In between helping the poor, whether local or from North Africa, Don Giorgio also helped the Gallieras after their eviction in 1993. Whenever he brought food and second-hand clothing to Igor and

Barbara, his volunteers would see him raise his eyes to the heavens. *Al dis na vrtà neanc per sbali,* he would say of Romano. He doesn't tell the truth even by accident. When the town of Finale Emilia threw the Gallieras onto the streets and Oddina Paltrinieri took in Dario, Don Giorgio cursed Romano's wicked ways but gave him yet another chance to redeem himself. He found him a modest country home on Via Abbà e Motto, which the Gallieras shared with a newly arrived Albanian family. Now that small child he barely remembered was threatening a life and a reputation he'd built with sweat and tears over the course of almost half a century—all in the span of an afternoon.

Meanwhile, prosecutors in Modena were slowly gathering evidence on Don Giorgio. They thought they'd found the dark side of a man who had long gone unnoticed by the law. After Dario, investigators had to wait a long time before Marta revealed what she knew about the shadowy sect. She started to talk on December 31, almost six months after she was taken away. The first of a long series of trials began in January 1998.

6.

When Lorena opened her door to me in Massa Finalese, she immediately struck me as a lively and friendly person. She had short hair, light-blue eyes, and plain clothes, and she wore no makeup. She was a woman devoted to God, who never had a bad word to say or made an off-color remark. Not even when, in tears, she told me the story of her long battle to get her children back.

Her three brothers were also there: Emidio, Giuliano, and Giuseppe Morselli. They'd spent years in prison after their nieces and nephews accused them of pedophilia. Enzo, Lorena's father, had also been sentenced to prison but died a few years earlier. The whole family had been devastated by the affair. Since 1998, six Morselli children had been taken away, and Lorena's sister-in-law, Monica, had died in prison. Her three brothers never recovered. Lingering anger and depression had left their mark. Now, these quiet, sullen men were over fifty years old, unmarried and childless. Their lives revolved around their mother, Lina, an energetic and combative eighty-year-old who, between 1998 and 1999, had lost her entire family and was now practically alone. Six grandchildren taken away, her husband and three sons arrested, and her daughter gone to France to avoid losing her youngest child. Now she was sitting at the table in her modest dining room, surrounded by pictures and letters she'd sent to her grandchildren over the years, all returned unopened.

"If you go looking for Veronica, my oldest grandchild," she said, giving me a tattered envelope, "please give her this letter."

But before I could go in search of anyone or anything, I needed court documents. I had to form my own opinion of the case, without being swayed by the tears of an elderly woman. After all, I didn't know anything about the Morselli family. They seemed like stand-up citizens, but they'd been accused of abusing children—their own children—and of torturing them physically and psychologically. This was the worst crime I could imagine. I couldn't and wouldn't allow myself to trust my first impressions; I had to uncover the truth.

"Come with me. I'll introduce you to someone," Lorena said at one point. We braved the whipping rain that had suddenly struck the plains and drove to a small church, the longtime headquarters of Finale Emilia's priest. Don Ettore Rovatti was an older man with a pleasant manner. He knew the case better than anyone. He'd followed it from the start. Meeting him was a real turning point. Don Ettore was the living archive of the trials and of everything that had been done, said, and written about them. He was obsessed with the case and had studied it in depth, poring over all the documents he could get his hands on. He remembered the names of all the main characters, as well as the month and year of each event. He also knew many of the people involved, including his friend Don Giorgio Govoni. He'd written a book about him after his death. It was titled *Don Giorgio Govoni: Martyr of Charity, Victim of Human Justice*. The few copies that were printed sold out. It did not go to a second printing because the publishers received threats from some of the children's lawyers. Don Ettore believed that the case was a hoax. The five trials that came of it resulted in several convictions, but they never proved anything except for the existence of an ancient war, now being waged on the backs of children, by the state against the church. Emilia Romagna represented the ideal place for such a clash, according to him, because past Communist administrations had infused an insensitive anticlerical ideology into the region's welfare and social services systems.

"There's a specific mindset behind all this legal posturing: that the family is always wrong, and the state is always right," Don Ettore told me, standing outside the old wooden doors of his church as evening descended on Finale Emilia. "These people want to destroy the family, just as Communism wanted to destroy private property. These AUSL psychologists and social workers want to prove that God, poor thing, doesn't know how to do his job. They think they know better than the Lord."

According to him, those sixteen children were taken away because of a witch hunt that rivaled the Inquisition of the fifteenth century, though with a different goal in mind, that of proving that the values imparted by the family—the most sacred Christian institution—are inferior and less effective than those taught by the state.

I wasn't convinced. Reports of sexual abuse, whether true—as prosecutors alleged—or false—as Don Ettore maintained—couldn't be boiled down to a power struggle between Communists and Catholics, no matter how prominent that struggle had been in the postwar era. I didn't know all the details of the case yet, but I expected that the logic behind it would either be simpler and more linear, or much more complex and multifaceted, than what I was hearing from this elderly priest in black garb, with a kind expression.

Don Ettore gave me a copy of his book. As soon as I started reading it, I realized my luck. This man had spent six years gathering and transcribing court documents with painstaking precision and deep resolve. He recorded everything in extreme detail, including dates, verdicts, reports, and personal data. Running more than three hundred pages, it was a detailed chronology, a handbook not meant for the casual reader but for whoever wanted to seriously look into the case. He presented a perfectly developed and clearly explained thesis, which was supported by documentation and plenty of references. There was no room for digression—each page adhered perfectly to what really happened and what had really been said. But his work did insist on a very clear hypothesis: that the children separated from their families between February 1997 and November 1998 had been taken due to a series of resounding errors in judgment on the part of social services and investigators, assisted by psychologist Valeria Donati and her colleagues. Don Ettore saw the matter as an incredible case of collective hysteria caused by the inexperience and incompetence of practitioners who thought they'd discovered a ring of pedophiles. Instead, they destroyed entire families. But Don Ettore was also a good friend of Don Giorgio and of several of the other suspects. Did his closeness to many of the actors cause him to overlook crucial details?

Early one morning, not long after our meeting, Don Ettore died of a heart attack. A few weeks later, his friend Antonella let me into his room on the second floor of the rectory. I was speechless. Don Ettore had lived in a small and spare room with an old, wooden single bed, two portraits of Jesus and one of Pope John Paul II hanging on the wall, and a large wooden armoire that took over an entire wall. Antonella opened the armoire. Inside were four shelves full of folders, each as thick as my outstretched hand and containing thousands of pages of verdicts from the court in Modena, the Court of Appeals in Bologna, and the Supreme Court of Cassation in Rome, as well as AUSL reports and documents. I sat down on Don Ettore's old mattress and stared at the mountain of paper. I called Alessia to let her know we had what we needed.

PART II

WHAT LIES BENEATH

7.

Alessia and I met Federico Scotta one evening at his apartment outside Bologna. He led us into a small, dimly lit room next to the kitchen. He shared the space with some college students—some of whom walked by as we talked, gave a weak *hello*, and left. I found out later that this wasn't really his house. He was only allowed to use the bathroom and kitchen. He was actually living in an old trailer parked in the garden. It was all he could afford on his salary as a part-time night watchman.

Federico was respectful and cordial, almost to a fault. All our phone calls had started and ended with *I'm sorry to have bothered you.* It was as if he was afraid to annoy or even hurt someone with his mere presence. Every time we talked, he compulsively raised both his hands and shrugged, as if trying to relieve us of the weight of his words. He'd preface every sentence with *If I remember correctly* or *Please excuse me, but I really don't remember.* He was a man who felt like a burden, always and to everyone.

I felt sorry for him. His gaunt features and the bags under his eyes were signs of harrowing, sleepless nights spent staring at a door. He was only two years older than I was, yet he looked much older than that. Life had crushed him. Since leaving prison in 2008, he'd lived off small jobs of little consequence, with agonizingly long shifts that paid €4.50 ($5.50) per hour, were renewed every three, six, or twelve months, but that eventually left him back on the street.

A few years after he finished serving his probation, he'd gone to work for a co-op delivering medical supplies to pharmacies across

Emilia Romagna. His delivery list contained the names of many towns and villages in the province of Modena. One of them was Sassuolo, but Federico didn't notice at first. When it came time to make the delivery, his blood froze, and he had a flashback to what had happened years before.

In the summer of 1997, when Elisa and Nick were taken away and Federico noticed the Post-it with the names and addresses of his children's new families, he'd memorized everything. Elisa had gone to a foster family near Mirandola. Nick's new family lived in the village he was heading to then. At the time, Federico knew that it was too risky to try to see his children immediately. So he'd dialed the Telecom Italia info line and given them the name of Nick's new family and the town in which they lived. Someone had told him that Nick's new parents owned a pharmacy. A few years before, he and Francesca had been arrested just for going to see Marta. He couldn't afford to make the same mistake again—and he didn't want to do anything that might traumatize the boy. He'd already lost custody of him. Then he was convicted of pedophilia, and, even if he'd wanted to visit, he would have had to wait until he'd served his time.

Prison spit him back out on to the street, depressed and afraid, thirty-three pounds lighter and with fewer teeth. Then fate put him in that van heading toward *that* town and *that* pharmacy. Federico parked near a tree-lined street, picked up the delivery, and went inside. It was Sunday and the store was empty, except for a young man in a blue Nike tracksuit. When their eyes met, Federico saw himself as a young man. This must be the baby boy he'd last seen seventeen years before, parked in a stroller in the Mirandola police station. Now he was smiling at him from behind a desk, sporting a black buzz cut and slightly almond-shaped eyes inherited from his mother, Kaempet.

"Is the owner here?" asked Federico.

"Not right now," the boy answered. "I'm his son. You can leave the package with me."

Federico smiled, thanked the boy, and left. Much later, he found out that that hadn't actually been Nick. Nick's new family did not own a pharmacy, but at the time, the effect was real. He climbed back into the van, drove a few hundred feet, pulled into an isolated parking space, and burst into tears. He was forty years old and had a prison term behind him and no future prospects. He was a failed man—he hadn't even been able to hold on to his family or even a job for more than a few years. His children had grown up in other families, and they had no idea who he was, nor did they want to have any contact with him. Federico lit a cigarette and thought about his life.

When the police arrived to take Elisa and Nick away, Federico was twenty-two years old and at the start of his career at a biomedical facility in Mirandola. But when news of his arrest appeared in the papers, his firm asked him to resign. Friends and colleagues distanced themselves from him. Without money for rent, Federico sent Kaempet to stay with relatives while he moved into a trailer. His grandmother supported him financially as he awaited trial.

Once pretrial investigations were over, his lawyer called him to his office in Mirandola. "Federico, I'm expecting a conviction," he said plainly. Federico was up against Dario's statement and the results of Elisa's and Marta's medical examinations. Prosecutors were on the warpath—the media, too—and it was all happening during a historic moment when the fight against pedophilia was becoming a full-on crusade. It was going to be hard to defend him. The prosecution had everything it needed to nail him to the wall along with his band of pedophiles. "Maybe we should consider a plea bargain," his lawyer concluded with a shrug. But a plea bargain was out of the question for Federico. He would face the trial and prove his innocence. He was sure of it. Just as he was sure that he'd be able to get his children back. He was young and cocky. But from the first hearings in January 1998, it became clear that things weren't going to go his way. Defense lawyers focused on the incompetence of Dr. Donati, who they said was too young and inexperienced for a complex case like this. They implied she'd strongly influenced Dario's testimony and, later, that of Elisa and Marta. They insisted there was no evidence that connected the "Massa group" (the Gallieras, Rosa, and Fredone) with the "Mirandola group" (the Scottas and Francesca).

On the other side of the courtroom, the prosecution uncovered a slew of evidence. Dario's drawings were shown to the court. They were a gallery of horrors, which left few doubts as to the existence of past trauma: children tied up and dead after suffering extreme agony; children locked in coffins; children with crushed heads; monsters with pointy ears holding daggers; a vampire with black wings growing out of its back, labeled "Ales." According to expert witnesses, the boy didn't have much of an imagination. He also had "no psychopathological signs," and while his stories were littered with gaps, hesitations, and reconsiderations, prosecutor Andrea Claudiani managed to convince the judges that he was credible. "Dario has revealed an enormous number of facts. He named people, places, families, houses, habits, cars and motorcycles, the colors of these, and precise and specific activities that have been confirmed by many people. He gave testimony on a multitude of terrifying and complex interconnected facts. He talked about undergoing oral relations, sodomy, sadomasochistic practices with iron and leather tools, and satanic rituals in which he was locked in a coffin. Dario's story was confirmed, as we've seen, an exceptional number of times. Should a few mistakes, insofar as they exist, undermine his credibility as a witness?"

And what court would believe a single word uttered by a Galliera? AUSL had investigated them thoroughly. A social worker had spoken to a fourteen-year-old from an underprivileged family in Massa who said he knew them and had participated in a sex party with Barbara and Adriana. It didn't matter that he later retracted his statement, along with the one where he said he knew of Fredone and his "passion for little girls." Police had found Polaroids at Fredone and Rosa's home. None of them were of Dario or acts of pedophilia, but a few showed Fredone in vulgar poses with a dildo, which was later found among his personal effects.

Dario wasn't the only one to mention Fredone, even though he called him Ales. Elisa had also named him. With the fragmented speech of a three-year-old, she told Dr. Donati about a house she went to with Federico, Marta, and Francesca to play with cats. She later drew cats covered in Band-Aids. There was more. Elisa's foster mother said the girl had once asked her to draw a naked man, and that when Elisa returned from her visits with her birth parents, she always had a rash on her butt. That was where Cristina Maggioni and her colleague Maurizio Bruni had later found suspicious scarring.

The judges soon realized that all the suspects "belonged to problematic families with financial difficulties and significant debts caused by subordinate cultural contexts," leading them to conclude that "they were not fully capable of appreciating how their behavior defied civilized society." In other words, Federico's and Romano's proclamations of a social services conspiracy were nothing but vain, pathetic attempts to escape the hurricane of evidence that would soon rain down on them and their accomplices. It was pointless to lie, to deny the proof. And who cares if Massa and Mirandola were two very different towns twelve miles apart, or that no one had proved that the Gallieras knew the Scottas or Francesca? The connection between the Massesi and Mirandolesi was undoubtedly there. Inspector Pagano discovered it after digging through their opaque pasts. Marta's mother, a fragile Neapolitan woman, had probably thrown herself off the balcony to avoid going to prison for abusing her daughter. Police archives revealed that some twenty years before, she'd worked as a prostitute at Bar Brennero in San

Prospero. The bar had closed long ago, but Pagano tracked down an ex-employee who confirmed he'd seen Don Giorgio eat there at least twice. There you go: the woman and the priest very likely knew each other. In fact, Dario said he'd seen Francesca at the home of that same Giorgio, the molester. The trucker-priest had evaded charges so far—he'd been brought into the case later—but prosecutors and the police were watching him closely, and sooner or later they'd catch him, too. Everything made sense. And it was all thanks to the confidence and poise of Dr. Donati, Dr. Burgoni, and Sister Annarita Ferrari of the Cenacolo Francescano.

On April 10, 1998, the prosecution closed the case. Romano, Adriana, and Igor Galliera, Rosa and Fredone, and Federico Scotta were sentenced to prison terms ranging from four to thirteen years. Dario's and Elisa and Nick's parents lost custody of their children.

Fredone kept up his usual bravado, but privately, he was not well. The charges and conviction had worn him down. The big man who used to terrorize the neighborhood by driving around town with dark sunglasses, always ready to break noses and give black eyes, was now anxious and emaciated. It was all too much, even for him. *Dio boia. Mi a so un putanièr, un làder, ma non so brísa un pedofil,* he'd told a friend. Fucking hell. He'd committed plenty of sins in his life, but he'd never laid hands on a child.

A few weeks after Fredone was sentenced to thirteen years in prison, his neighbors noticed a large limb poking out from behind the balcony railing on the second floor of his home in Massa. Fredone had collapsed onto the floor and was breathing heavily. When the ambulance arrived, EMTs broke down the door and found him facedown on the ground without a pulse. The second dead person connected to the case in seven months. But not the last.

8.

Around nine fifteen a.m. on March 16, 1998, a few weeks before the end of the trial, a car arrived from Mirandola and parked in front of Carlo Alberto Dalla Chiesa, Massa Finalese's elementary school. Two police officers, Dr. Valeria Donati, and social worker Maria Teresa Mambrini climbed out. They entered the building and met with the school's principal. The police were carrying a protection order for a child in 3B. The principal led them to a room next to a classroom. A girl with light-brown hair was waiting for them. Her name was Margherita Giacco. Two teachers were with her.

The adults conferred with each other, then Dr. Donati and Ms. Mambrini sat down to talk to Margherita. They explained that she wouldn't be returning home that day. They would be taking her somewhere safe because they wanted to understand a few things about her family.

A teacher tried to comfort Margherita as she began to cry. "Margherita, don't worry. We'll be waiting for you." Then Margherita got into the police car, which took her to a small town in southern Reggio Emilia. Social services had found her a foster home associated with the Cenacolo Francescano. A couple in their fifties, Lara and Giovanni, managed the home. They'd made foster care their mission. They lived in a big, two-story house with several other kids, all older than Margherita. Giovanni was a teacher nearing retirement, and Lara had decided to be a housewife so she could look after children—their own and the ones they took in. She was used to being around children with all sorts of problems, but Margherita's arrival worried her. New arrivals usually joined the family gradually to minimize the trauma of changing homes. But in this case, they hadn't been given fair warning. They simply received a request to look after the child for six months. At first, Lara had said, "No, we can't, I'm sorry." After almost twenty years, she and her husband wanted to dial back their foster care activities. But then, AUSL had called again. This was an emergency. Could she stay at least one month? "OK, we can do a month." Not more. And that girl's story wasn't simple. The two social workers who spoke to Lara a few days before had been candid and told her that, based on some of the things Margherita had said, they believed she'd been the victim of severe abuse, even though there was no proof yet. But after the initial orientation, Lara breathed a sigh of relief. Margherita was friendly and calm, and she seemed to appreciate their big, extended family. Dr. Donati immediately set up a schedule of visits to her office. She also asked Lara to listen carefully to everything Margherita said and to encourage her to talk, since Margherita struggled to talk during sessions.

A week after the removal, on a spring day marked by an unseasonable snowfall, Lara brought Margherita to Milan to meet Dr. Maggioni. Lara was anxious. Before leaving, Dr. Donati and Ms. Mambrini had specifically asked Margherita, "Do you think someone hurt you?" She had replied, "I don't know," an answer they found suspicious. Dr. Maggioni was nice and considerate. She made sure Margherita felt comfortable. She showed her the instrument she was going to use, calling it "a sort of telescope," and examined the girl with courtesy and care. She met with no resistance. Once the visit was over, Dr. Maggioni leaned toward Margherita. "Yes, someone has hurt you," she said. "But don't worry, because what happened in the past won't affect your future. You'll be able to have children."

Once back in the car and heading down the A1 toward Bologna, toward home, Margherita finally seemed to relax. They stopped at a rest stop, and Lara left her in the warm car, braving the snow to get her something to eat. They got back on the road, and a few minutes later, Margherita was fast asleep. The stress and anxiety of that week must have been hard on her.

Mirandola's social services, Bologna's juvenile court, and the Modena district attorney's office had been secretly following Margherita's case for two months. Everything started at a quarter past noon on January 22, 1998, in the school courtyard in Massa Finalese. The bell had just rung, and as one of Margherita's teachers was leaving, she ran into Antonia, the mother of a student. Antonia wanted to speak privately about a very serious matter involving her daughter's friend and classmate. The two girls lived in the same building in the projects on Via Volta and often played together. She and her daughter, Tania, lived on the third floor, Margherita on the second. But Tania had started to tell her mother that Margherita did and said strange things while they were playing. She was in the habit of taking the clothes off her Big Jims and Barbies and arranging the dolls in vulgar positions while making strange noises and using inappropriate language for a nine-year-old girl. Margherita even told Tania that she'd seen one of her older brothers have oral sex with his girlfriend. Antonia had become suspicious. This girl often ate at her table and accepted rides to school from her in the morning. Antonia tried to talk to Maria, Margherita's mother, but she didn't take the matter very seriously. She responded that since Margherita often slept in the big bed with her and her husband, Santo, she might have glimpsed something on TV. Santo watched movies in bed until late at night. But Antonia wasn't convinced. She decided to talk to Margherita's teachers, who referred the matter to Principal Giovanni Maccaferri.

Mr. Maccaferri knew the Giaccos well. They were a large family from Campania who had been living in Massa for many years. Their children had gone to his elementary school. But he also remembered

Margherita for another reason. Three years before, in 1995, when she was in first grade, she had racked up absences from school, some of them for long periods of time. Mr. Maccaferri summoned her parents. They told him she was hospitalized for a bit, and then they'd had to go down south a few times and had brought Margherita with them. By the end of the year, Margherita had been absent for half the school year, causing her to be left back. But nothing changed. The unexplained absences continued, and Margherita was always behind.

Mr. Maccaferri decided to call Dr. Burgoni, the head of social services. AUSL intervened to evaluate Margherita's situation. They found that she had "developmental disturbances in language and academic abilities due to a situation of cultural deprivation." Margherita was only able to express herself in Neapolitan dialect, so she was assigned a special needs teacher. This was the teacher Antonia had approached. Antonia had also been concerned that the Giaccos often took Margherita to a pub where a "gay" singer performed. No wonder Margherita was too tired to get up at seven a.m. and go to school the next morning. And God knows what kind of movies she watched in bed with her parents. And when she played with Tania, she told Tania about her brother's "willy" and taught her to make "love sounds."

Mr. Maccaferri wrote a report for the Mirandola police saying that "Margherita is used to watching pornographic films at home with her parents or brother." The report ended up on the desk of the Modena district attorney, who was already prosecuting the pedophiles who had abused Dario, Elisa, Nick, and Marta. And here was another case, again in Massa Finalese. But this wasn't the only thing to pique the investigators' interest: the Giacco family lived in the same projects in Via Volta from which the Galliera family had been evicted in 1993, and where little Dario had taken his first steps. Santo and Romano had been neighbors and had known one another. Inspector Pagano started to investigate.

Santo and Maria Giacco had moved to the Bassa from the Naples area in 1976. Santo was born in Afragola, Maria in Casavatore, two very poor towns blighted by the Camorra. They'd met when she was thirteen and he was seventeen. After going out for two years, they'd had a *scappatella*, forcing their families to accept their relationship by getting knocked up, and she went to stay at his parents' house. The families immediately met to plan the wedding. Maria was pregnant with their first daughter, and she was only sixteen. At twenty, she and Santo were on a train to Modena in search of a better life.

In Emilia Romagna, Santo cultivated a handlebar mustache and found work as a mason. He soon established a small construction business. Things were going well and money was coming in, even though his betting on horses sometimes weighed on the family's finances. Maria, a small woman with jet-black hair, spent most of her time cooped up at home. She never went out alone. She got lost, confused, and agitated on her own. She didn't drive and couldn't even ride a bike. And anyway, she had too much to do inside, where the family was growing and growing. They were far from their native land, but the Giaccos had managed to recreate their own little Neapolitan microcosm in the heart of the Pianura Padana. The kids mostly spoke dialect. Margherita, the youngest of six children, was born in 1989. She was the most spoiled. Maria let her sleep with her and Santo in the big bed and often let her stay home from school. Maria had never gone to school and couldn't read, and her attitude toward Margherita's education was just as casual as it had been for her other children: school was a place to go to only if there was time. She didn't like to get Margherita up early in the morning, so she let her sleep in. She didn't care about the absences or about what the teachers thought.

The other Giacco children were all grown up and some of them had children of their own. One of Margherita's brothers had had a few run-ins with the law, but other than that, the family had never drawn the attention of the authorities. But now, the Mirandola police wanted to understand what was going on in that house. In particular, they wanted to know what was in those videos Antonia had mentioned. So they came up with a plan. They showed up at the Giacco home just after lunch, about a month after Margherita's school had alerted them to the problem. Santo was coming out of the shower when he noticed police lights. They were coming from the courtyard. When he looked out the window and saw five or six squad cars, he thought someone had killed themselves. But then they rang his doorbell. He and Maria were suspects in a robbery, they said. "Someone saw you walk into the store as your wife waited in the car."

Santo looked at them as if they were crazy.

"Maybe you saw this in a movie? My wife doesn't even have her license."

The officers didn't care. They were there to search the house. "Mr. Giacco, where is your weapon?" an officer asked.

"I'm a plasterer, not a gunsmith," responded the mason of Afragola, with his usual arrogant sarcasm.

"This is no time to be funny."

As he waited for the search to end, Santo noticed that they were taking his video collection. These were mostly action movies and Hollywood blockbusters. What did they have to do with a robbery? As they sorted through a pile of videos in the garage, they found one with a naked woman on the cover. Santo's son told the police it was his. Santo shrugged—anyone could have a video like that. And again: What did it have to do with a robbery? Two hours later, Santo was taken to the police station in Mirandola. He returned home late that night, certain that this unpleasant misunderstanding would soon be over.

When Margherita vanished from school a month later, her parents didn't make the connection between the two events. In fact, they were sure someone had kidnapped her. They didn't understand who these social workers and psychologists were, talking about precautionary distancing and asking Maria and Santo to attend weekly meetings. They especially didn't understand that new word everyone was saying. *Petophonia. Pedophonia.* Never heard of it.

"It's when somebody rapes a child," they were told.

Santo still didn't understand. "I thought that was a *maníeco*."

One evening in midspring, Lara and Margherita were alone in the dining room after dinner. Margherita had been living with Lara for more than two months, and little by little, she'd started to trust her. Lara was a kind and mild-mannered woman and had welcomed Margherita into her home. Margherita had asked to speak to her in private. One time, she confided, someone had hurt her. It was someone in a bar in Finale Emilia. Her parents often went there to visit her brother, who lived above the bar. Sometimes, when they went up to see him, they left her downstairs to play video games. Alone. One day, a man had taken her to the bathroom and touched her down there.

"Who was this man?" Lara asked.

"He was the one who brought the coffee."

Probably the bartender. And what was the name of the bar?

"I don't remember. La Torre . . . Maybe Il Castello."

Lara flipped through the Modena phone book. Finale Emilia pages. Bar. There was one that was called La Corte del Re.

"Yes, yes, that's the one," said Margherita.

Lara was upset. She asked Margherita to write everything down. Maybe it would help her remember. She knew there was something Margherita still wasn't telling her.

"There are things about her dad that she doesn't want to say, that she can't say," Dr. Donati had told Lara after one of Margherita's sessions. "If she tells you about them, please let me know."

Margherita wrote in her diary that she'd seen this mysterious man talk to her father. Her dad scared her. Once, when they were alone in her parents' room and her mother wasn't there, he'd even shown her a porno. For this and for other reasons that she still wasn't able to talk about, she absolutely did not want to see him or return to her family.

She still hadn't accused anyone in her family of abusing her, but it was only a matter of time. The social workers in Mirandola knew this. After a traumatic event, children experience a psychic block that can last for weeks or even months. For Margherita, it had been two months, for Dario three, and for Marta six. Nothing could be more normal. After all, they'd been living in an upside-down world where the people who were supposed to love and protect them were actually trying to hurt them. And even though they were old enough to distinguish between right and wrong, they still didn't have all the intellectual and emotional tools to understand and articulate what had happened.

The trick was to gain their trust and provide a friendly environment where they'd be encouraged to remember and talk. This would allow psychologists to pierce through the armor of their seemingly impenetrable verbal and physical defenses, the *I don't knows* and the *I don't remembers*. The trick was to persevere and to help the children find the courage and strength to tell the truth. To take the burden off their shoulders. So they could feel better. And who knows, maybe even forget. The key was to insist. Sometimes by asking softly, sometimes more forcefully. But insist nonetheless. The first revelations would be hesitant, almost imperceptible. Then the terrible and shameful tales would pour out. And their parents, who tried to seem so proper in AUSL meetings, would be outed for what they really were. They called it "recovered memory therapy," and it was widely used by psychologists at the Children's Institute and the National Center on Child Abuse and Neglect in the United States. The institution claims the method helped them identify hundreds of serial abusers.

Dr. Donati, a thirty-year-old psychologist who'd started working for the AUSL as an intern only four years before, had displayed a rare talent among her peers. Despite her young age and limited experience, she had the ability to read people and situations and to sense when a silence—*that* type of silence—was hiding a dark world where only strong souls would dare to tread. She was the primary instigator of this case. Dario, Elisa, Nick, Marta, and Margherita were safe now and would someday be grateful for her indomitable will and her relentlessness. And even if the parents accused her of planting words and who knows what else into the minds of their children for who knows what personal reasons, Dr. Maggioni's medical exams had confirmed her suspicions. Valeria, as the children called her, was the skeleton key that could open the door to every child, tiptoe into the dark corners of their subconscious, spot their trauma, and unblock their defenses, allowing them to unburden themselves and feel better.

The prosecution thought Dr. Donati was a brave woman, and her testimony had been instrumental in crushing the defense. The judges mentioned her in their verdict, praising her "competence and balance." Court experts had evaluated the children's statements with a method called criteria-based content analysis, which is used to ascertain the reliability and truthfulness of abuse victim testimony. It uses a set of indicators, including logical structure, spontaneous correction, self-deprecation, and quantity of realistic details, like descriptions of physical sensations tied to the abuse. These evaluations also confirmed Dr. Donati's interpretations.

Dr. Burgoni had put together a team of psychologists and social workers to support her. Together with the police, juvenile court, and the prosecution, they formed a brigade designed to flush out pedophiles near and far, all the way up to the demonic parent organization they were sure was operating in some Italian or European city, financed and cloaked by secret overlords who were so powerful that they'd managed to extend their tentacles even to the small country roads of the Bassa.

Reports out of Belgium around that time seemed to confirm these suspicions. Just two years before, in February 1996, Belgians had learned about Marc Dutroux, the monster of Marcinelle. He was arrested with his wife for raping six girls, four of whom had died. His case was a worldwide story, and shocking details continued to emerge in the months following his arrest. Dutroux had already been arrested in 1985 for kidnapping and raping five teenagers, and although a court had sentenced him to thirteen years in solitary confinement in 1989, he was released in 1992. Before they finally rearrested him, authorities ignored evidence that could have saved the lives of at least two girls. They were found beaten to death. The authorities' investigations had been so superficial and so lacking as to create the legitimate impression that they were the accomplices and enablers of a homicidal maniac. A few months after Dutroux's arrest, almost three hundred thousand people poured into downtown Brussels to demand justice, brandishing banners saying "They're Everywhere, Let's Find Them!"

Echoes of this scandal rebounded across the Italian press throughout 1997 and 1998, when news of another case, also in Belgium, emerged, this time involving 340 children. But these weren't the only cases that worried prosecutors and police around the world. The internet was making online chat rooms widely accessible, as well as facilitating the selling of images and videos of children of all ages through illegal pornographic sites. Until then, child pornography had been confined to the trafficking of VHS tapes in closed groups. Now, it was becoming accessible to an increasing number of users. And the selection seemed to be growing exponentially. The papers were running stories about it more and more. And prosecutors in northern Italy, especially in Milan, were the first line of defense in the war on pedophiles. District attorneys like Pietro Forno were leading the charge.

Meanwhile, in Finale Emilia, the police were busy trying to identify the man who'd molested Margherita. They knew he wore a funny-looking hat that fell over his ears and that people called him "Giuly."

9.

An unusually intense heat wave hit Italy and most of Europe in the summer of 1998. Thursday, July 2, was one of the most scorching days of all, with temperatures reaching record highs. It was a big day in soccer, too, and people were eagerly awaiting the World Cup quarterfinals. France was hosting the tournament, and the Italian national team was about to face them at the Stade de France the following day.

Around nine thirty a.m., the phone in a country home in Pavignane, near Massa Finalese, started to ring. A thirty-seven-year-old ceramic worker named Giuliano Morselli picked up. It was Mrs. Benati, the head of the AUSL social services in Mirandola.

"Mr. Morselli, we've had to move up tomorrow's meeting," she said. "Please come by with your daughter this morning. We'll be waiting for you."

Giuliano sighed and called to his eight-year-old daughter, Cristina. She had brown hair and a high forehead and wore big, round glasses.

"Let's go. They're waiting for us in Mirandola."

Cristina understood immediately and ran off to hide under her bed and cry.

"Come on, get out of there," her father said, trying to cajole her. But she wouldn't budge, and she kept crying. After a few more unsuccessful attempts to talk her down, Giuliano dragged her out by the arm. He was crying, too. During the fifteen-minute ride from Pavignane to Mirandola, Giuliano and his wife, Monica Roda, tried to calm their daughter. Mommy and Daddy had a few problems to resolve, Giuliano explained. Social services were going to put Cristina in the care of another family, but just for a little while. They'd visit her whenever they could until things got better.

Giuliano and Monica were both from Massa Finalese. They'd been married for almost ten years, but they hadn't been getting along lately. Childhood meningitis had left Monica with a fragile disposition—she suffered from several physical problems and insecurity. After Cristina came Riccardo, who was born prematurely at seven months and had psychomotor delays. Monica's postnatal recovery had been difficult. She'd long suffered from sporadic epileptic seizures, but they had intensified and were now accompanied by violent mood swings that she sometimes took out on Cristina. Monica was afraid of having another crisis while Giuliano was at work at the factory. It had already happened once, when she and Cristina were alone. Since the new baby needed constant attention, they asked Giuliano's mother, Lina, to take care of him.

Around the same time, Monica and Cristina had moved in with Monica's mother. They went home to stay with Giuliano only on weekends. The arrangement caused more than a bit of friction. Giuliano hated it, and he hated his mother-in-law, who reciprocated the feeling. He wanted Monica and Cristina home in Pavignane more often, but his wife's deteriorating health impelled him to give in.

On top of all that was happening at home, Cristina was struggling with language acquisition and required the intervention of Mirandola's child neuropsychiatry unit. Her speech therapist, Dr. Veronesi, immediately noticed the hardship affecting her family and believed it was partly due to Monica. Riccardo's birth and constant need for attention had exacerbated Cristina's anxiety. She seemed to think that no one wanted her or loved her. So, Dr. Veronesi suspended speech therapy and assigned Cristina to a colleague, Dr. Emma Avanzi, warning her that the girl suffered from "significant psychological discomfort and a depressive nature, with fears of abandonment and generalized anxiety."

Dr. Avanzi carefully observed Cristina. She thought she looked "spent." Cristina showed no initiative, she was sad, she had no self-esteem, and she thought she was ugly. Sometimes, during her visits, she behaved "strangely." She was nervous and restless and always wanted to go to the bathroom. When she played games with other children on the mat, she'd sit in an odd position with her "legs open." She also told some very bizarre stories of monsters and torture, along the lines of Hansel and Gretel. But Cristina's stories "never ended." There was never a resolution, never a positive outcome.

Dr. Avanzi believed Cristina's real problem was her mother. Between her angry outbursts and excessive doting on Riccardo, she was clearly neglecting Cristina. Cristina seemed to be closer to her father, but her posture and facial expression when talking about him suggested she was holding something back. She didn't show enthusiasm even when she told Dr. Avanzi about the time her father took her to see *Titanic* in the theater, or about the presents he gave her. But what worried Dr. Avanzi the most was that in two years of speech therapy, Cristina hadn't made any progress. In fact, she'd regressed significantly. A "normal" child wouldn't break down in tears like she did during religion or catechism lessons. A "normal" child couldn't possibly make up stories about monsters and mean parental figures living in a LEGO house, where there were three beds placed side by side and bars on the windows, and where someone was going "pee-pee" and "poo-poo," where there was blood, where people were using "medical tubes," and where Daddy looked at her funny when she took a bath.

Dr. Avanzi turned to her colleagues at social services for help. They introduced her to Dr. Donati. Dr. Avanzi had heard of Dr. Donati's work with the children of Massa and Mirandola, so she told her about Cristina. She didn't have an intellectual disability, and she wasn't psychotic or delirious, but she'd still given Dr. Avanzi concern, prompting her to ask for help. "I've been in this job for sixteen years and I've never seen anything like this. What do you think?"

They decided to place Cristina in temporary foster care. Move her to neutral ground, away from familial interference, so they could properly look into the situation. Mother, father, and daughter arrived at the AUSL offices in Mirandola and went up to social services. Giuliano looked around. He'd been told he'd be meeting the family that was going to take care of his daughter for a few days, but no one was there. The Morsellis sat down in Monica Benati's office to sign some papers. Cristina was left in another room to play. When they emerged, she was gone. At first, the Morsellis didn't understand what was happening. Then, in the hallway, they ran into Lina. She was in tears. They'd called her in, too, along with Riccardo. They said it was serious, and they had to bring him in for a medical exam.

On July 2, Cristina moved in with a family who lived in a nearby town. Gilda, her foster mother, was a doctor involved in social work. She immediately saw that something was wrong with the girl. Cristina's hair was greasy, as if she hadn't washed it in a long time. In general, Cristina didn't seem very healthy. She seemed neglected. She was ignorant of the basic rules of hygiene, and she didn't know how to sit at a table or how to be around people. And when she had to change, she locked herself in her room, terrified that the boys in the family might see her. At night, her sleep was restless. She said she sometimes dreamed about her father molesting her and doing things to her down there while her mom hid behind the bedroom door listening. A few days later, a social worker brought her to Milan to see Dr. Maggioni. Exam results confirmed the psychologists' suspicions. There were lesions. Someone had hurt her.

Giuliano and Monica didn't understand. No one was telling them where their children were or when they could visit them or when they'd return. A few days after the children were taken away, they received a decree from the juvenile court in Bologna that said Cristina might have undergone "severely detrimental behavior within the family," which was why custody was being suspended for two months without visiting rights. Cristina and Riccardo were separated and assigned to different families.

Giuliano asked his eldest sister, Lorena, for help. She was the second of the five Morselli children. Giuliano was the third, and he and Lorena were born only nineteen months apart. But while their ages didn't do much to set them apart, their personalities did. Lorena had always been the dominant one: the one who decided, the one who organized, and the one who kept everyone in line—including the oldest, Emidio—while their parents were working shifts at the factory or picking fruit in the fields.

She was the one he turned to whenever he had a problem. Lorena Morselli was short, with short brown hair and bright-blue eyes. She was a determined, scrappy woman. When she learned that social services had taken her niece and nephew, she was shocked. What right did they have? After a few days without news of Cristina, Lorena picked up the phone and called Mirandola for an explanation. Her conversation with social worker Odette Magri was a waste of time. Lorena was furious. She knew her niece's removal was a hard blow for her brother and sister-in-law. And though Lorena only saw them for birthdays and important events and disapproved of the excessively severe tone Monica sometimes used with Cristina, she pitied the woman. She was fragile, insecure, and still more of a daughter than a mother.

Lorena went to the AUSL offices in person. She fought. But it didn't do any good. Cristina had been taken away because Dr. Avanzi suspected she was being abused, so they had to wait and see. "After all, Mrs. Morselli, children never lie."

10.

Dr. Donati's investigations were beginning to bear fruit. She and her team were rooting out the other members of the ring, one by one. At least twelve people had been identified so far. And there were many more suspects to go. The existence of the band of pedophiles was no longer in doubt. The police drew a web of connections over a map of the area.

But no one had been able to corroborate the satanic rituals Dario had mentioned. Elisa Scotta was too young to offer accurate or credible testimony, and Marta, Margherita, and Cristina hesitated to confirm the story. They didn't remember. Or maybe they were too afraid of what would happen to them if they talked.

As the summer of 1998 approached, Dario spoke again. He told Mrs. Tonini about another time those two disturbing characters—Giorgios One and Two—had come to see him at school. They'd had no problem entering (a janitor helped them), but this time, they hadn't taken him anywhere. They waited for him in his empty classroom during recess. Then Dario heard someone calling his name. It was Rita Spinardi, his teacher. "Come here, Dario, your friends are here," she said, tugging him along.

He didn't understand. What friends? Why was his teacher treating him like that? As soon as he went in, Dario's heart skipped a beat.

Giorgio One went up to him and kissed him. Dario kicked the man to break free. Rita became angry and slapped him. She ordered him to go sit at his desk, next to Giorgio Two. Outside, his classmates continued to play. Reluctant and afraid, Dario sat down. Rita was his teacher and their accomplice. Best to obey her and wait for them to leave. Once again, he heard the message loud and clear: *Keep your mouth shut, or bad things will happen to you and your new family.*

Mrs. Tonini had trouble believing him at first. Rita? What did she have to do with it? How did she know those men? They most likely came from the Bassa Modenese, some forty minutes away from Mantova. How extensive was this network? Romano Galliera was a part of it, as were those other disgusting people who'd terrorized and put their hands on her foster son. But who else? Did they really have so many followers?

Dario said Rita had let them in more than once. Like the time he went to the bathroom and ran into them there. They made him stand still as they slapped him so hard he spit blood. Mrs. Tonini remembered that Dario had come home from school one day complaining about a cut in his mouth. When she'd asked Rita about it, she'd played it down.

"He probably just bit his tongue eating or playing."

It had been that damned Giorgio once again, the monster that gave Dario nightmares every night. Rita was covering for him. She was on his side. Rita was his "girlfriend." She was mean to Dario. She'd punished him more than once. She slapped him and made him stand with his face against a column or with his hands in the air. She called him a liar and confiscated his planner after she'd seen him drawing Giorgio One and Giorgio Two. Rita wasn't the woman Mrs. Tonini thought she was. But now everything made sense. She was always minimizing events, saying she never saw anything happen, that she never noticed Dario's obvious discomfort. It was all part of the diabolical plan she was a part of. And also, it explained why some of the pages of Dario's planner were missing.

Rita wasn't in school during this period. She was being hospitalized for a very difficult operation. When she was released, a colleague went to pick her up.

"Rita, I have to tell you something," her colleague said. "The police are looking for you. I think it has something to do with Dario. I wanted to tell you before they showed up at your door."

Rita was still weak from her operation. She didn't understand.

"What do they want from me?" she asked. "In twenty-eight years of teaching I've never had a problem with anyone."

She returned home exhausted and threw herself on the bed. She woke up with a fever of 104°F to the sound of someone ringing the doorbell. It was Inspector Pagano from the Mirandola police. He claimed to have spoken to parents at Dario's school who told him she had inflicted corporal punishment on the children. She made them stand with their hands up, sometimes for hours, or she pulled them by the hair and slapped them hard in the face. Now he was on her doorstep holding a warrant for her arrest.

Rita wasn't the only one to receive a visit from the police. A few weeks later, a convoy of squad cars arrived at Don Giorgio Govoni's two rectories, in Staggia and San Biagio. They had search warrants. The prosecution had decided it was time to show its cards. From Modena to Ferrara, even the rocks knew that the trucker-priest had something to do with all of this.

The don wasn't home. They stopped him nearby, as he was driving his white Fiorino. Back in the apartment, Inspector Pagano leaned on a shelf containing two volumes of the *Encyclopedia of Love*. Before confiscating them, he leafed through one and noticed drawings of people having sex. He moved on to a room full of different types and colors of shoes.

"Are these yours?" Pagano asked Don Giorgio, indicating a pair of beige boots with heels. Don Giorgio nodded. Pagano confiscated them immediately. They matched Dario's description. And what about the two women's carnival masks he found in a broom closet with some other trinkets? What were they doing at the home of a priest? Police also found several sets of keys in a drawer. They opened the homes Don Giorgio was managing. Four of them belonged to the house the Gallieras lived in after their eviction, when they shared a house with the Albanian family. They were labeled "Romano house," "Romano kitchen," "Igor's room," and "Albanian children's room." The inspector confiscated those as well.

Then he noticed nine checkbooks for nine different accounts. There were also quite a few receipts for government bonds valued between 5,000,000 lira ($3,000) and 100,000,000 lira ($62,000). He'd recently paid about 40,000,000 lira ($25,000) to a certain Emer. Probably an Albanian. Something wasn't right. It was suspicious that a country priest should be dealing with all that money, have all those bank accounts, and be managing all that housing. Who cares that he also owned a transportation company? A quick search with the Automobile Club d'Italia turned up forty-seven license plates in his name. A huge number.

There was a computer on the desk. "Is this yours?" police asked the priest.

"Someone gave it to me."

An officer turned it on and checked the search history. Three recent searches: *little girl, hard, friends of children.* Don Giorgio Govoni was in trouble.

A week before the Ferragosto holiday, in a session with Dr. Donati at the Cenacolo Francescano, Marta spoke again. Almost a year had gone by since her mother had thrown herself off the balcony, and eight months had passed since Marta had finally talked about going to apartments where strange men molested her. This time, she told Dr. Donati that her mother used to bring her to a cemetery, where she saw people wearing white and black robes that touched the ground. The adults had "dug open" a grave and shown her a corpse that had "a bloody face" and was missing an arm. The body belonged to "a man who had hurt" her. Then the grown-ups traumatized her even further by explaining that corpses can come back to life. Marta also remembered seeing a lot of skulls, "the real kind," laid out around her while "they were hurting" her. She couldn't name the place where all this happened or point to it on a map. But she knew that she wasn't the only little girl at those satanic rituals. Dr. Donati immediately went to the district attorney's office to talk to Claudiani. Here at last was the confirmation of what Dario had said months ago. The events Marta described were the same. It couldn't be a coincidence.

In September, the Giaccos and the Morsellis asked social services and the juvenile court if they could see their children—Margherita, Cristina, and little Riccardo. They were told it wasn't possible. The authorities still had to "get a better idea" of what had happened. The girls, meanwhile, had returned to school in their new towns and attended regular meetings with Dr. Donati and Dr. Avanzi. Although they didn't verbalize it, they seemed increasingly unhappy and anxious. Their behavior exhibited several concerning indicators.

One day, while Cristina was doing her history homework, she had a hysterical fit after reading a chapter on Christian catacombs and burial rites. Gilda didn't know what to do. Her catechism teacher had also mentioned an incident that had happened one afternoon when she was talking to the children about the Devil. Cristina had started to scream. *No, the Devil doesn't exist, there was no Devil, the Devil couldn't take children away.*

Margherita also seemed to be obsessed with the idea of the Devil. She was convinced it was a living creature that was hiding in the world. She talked about it with any adult who would listen—with her teacher, with a priest she'd confessed to, with the nuns at the Cenacolo, with her foster mother. And with Dr. Donati, who sensed that Margherita's fear of being taken by the Devil was a form of misdirection designed to avoid talking about what really happened to her at home with Mommy and Daddy.

"You often talk about the Devil," she said. "Maybe you saw him somewhere?"

Margherita spread her fingers and looked her straight in the eye. "Finally, you get it."

During the last week of October 1998, three of the seven children who'd been taken from their parents made revelations that marked a turning point for the prosecution. Dario was the first to speak. The abuses suffered at home and in cemeteries were only part of the story. There was more. One night, during a ritual he'd participated in when he was only six, he'd murdered someone. His father put a knife in his hand and forced him to kill an "Albanian boy." The grown-ups then "stitched him up" and returned the boy to his mother, but she looked at them as if they were crazy. What was she supposed to do with a dead boy? He was useless. So the satanic acolytes cut him up and burned him in the fireplace. Investigators were stunned. Dario's stories had been leading them down a dark pit for months. Now they'd found the bottom. The ultimate goal of the sect was to commit murder. To feel the thrill of that extreme perversion, to be as evil as possible. There was no other explanation. And if they'd been able to force a child to commit such a vile act, they must have done it themselves, too. Pagano and his colleagues started rooting through missing person archives. But if the victims were foreigners, as it seemed they were, it was going to be very hard to find them.

Then, Margherita "unburdened herself" of the memories she'd been holding on to for months. It was true, Santo had hurt her. He'd taken her to "bad places" where children were forced to dress up in robes and masks. He took her to the Finale Emilia cemetery and to the Castello delle Rocche, a castle that dated back to the fifteenth century and was situated in the center of town. That was where they hid the robes for the rituals. The grown-ups dressed up as devils and forced the little ones to say "bad things about Jesus." Parents treated the children like merchandise. They traded them for sex acts among the headstones.

Cristina's testimony was even more damning and involved practically her whole family. In addition to abusing her repeatedly, her mom and dad had also made her little body available to the entire Morselli family. Grandpa Enzo, Giuliano, and paternal uncles Emidio and Giuseppe all came to her house outside Pavignane almost every night, sometimes dragging her out of bed to abuse her. A family of depraved maniacs. They'd obviously been severely neglected growing up, causing them to be more like beasts than human beings. But even then, what kind of a beast would allow its offspring to be treated so cruelly? The Morsellis killed cats and forced Cristina to drink their blood; sometimes they "injected" it directly into her. Other times, they forced her into a car and took her to dark alleys around town. Almost every night. Cristina said the children were "packed into" a line of cars that took up the whole road and then were taken to the cemetery. Not the one in Finale Emilia that Margherita had mentioned but the one in Cristina's village, Massa Finalese. She got there by car. Once at the gate, the adults threw ropes over the side and climbed up, then helped the children over. Inside, people were wearing priest robes with "devil hoods." Cristina couldn't remember how many people were there. She couldn't even remember their faces. The "leader" was her uncle Emidio, Giuliano's older brother. The children were abused and then subjected to rituals meant to turn them into the "children of the Devil," so they could "rule the world." This was the same story Dario had told months before when he'd talked about the "fake funeral" and exhumations. Cristina, too, felt a deep sense of guilt for having hurt animals.

Dr. Avanzi listened. She'd been born and raised in Massa Finalese. Some of her relatives were buried in that cemetery. Cristina had drawn a map, depicting the cemetery's main gate and the side entrance by the parking lot. She seemed to know it well. Then she revealed a new detail that seemed to confirm Dario's and Marta's accounts: the exchange of money. Giuliano and Monica had received "a lot" from uncle Emidio, probably as payment for Cristina.

One of the Black Mass officiants was a priest, but Cristina couldn't remember his name. Maybe Pietro. Don Pietro. And there were other children with her in the cemetery, including four of her aunt Lorena's children: Veronica, Pietro, Federico, and Aurora. Giuliano brought them there. But he did it without their parents knowing. He would pick them up in the afternoon, telling Lorena he was taking them to play with Cristina. Then he would bring them home late at night, telling Lorena that the kids had fallen asleep at his house.

Social services was in an uproar. Even if Mrs. Morselli had no idea her entire family belonged to a group of maniacal Devil worshippers, what kind of mother would let her children stay out on so many weeknights until such a late hour? And how did she not see that they had been traumatized? Social services informed the district attorney, who asked the Mirandola police to look into it. By now, it wasn't easy to keep a low profile in Massa Finalese. Police had already carried out searches and inspections on the Gallieras, Fredone, Rosa, and the Giaccos. They'd tried and failed to find the names and addresses of other accomplices Dario said belonged to his father's gang.

The Morsellis were a big family, and they were well known, but they were also close to Don Giorgio Govoni. Enzo, the patriarch, was a respected elder in Massa. Emidio was a supermarket manager. Giuliano was more introverted, but after marrying Monica, enmity between their two families had become the subject of conversation and gossip. Giuseppe, the youngest brother, played in three musical groups that performed at local clubs. Lorena was a daycare teacher who was very active in the church. She and her husband, Delfino, participated in most church activities.

Lorena was an institution in Massa Finalese. At thirty-nine, and with almost twenty years of daycare experience under her belt, she'd watched hundreds of local children grow up. She knew their families. She and Delfino volunteered with UNITALSI, the National Italian Union for the Transport of the Sick to Lourdes and International Sanctuaries. Lorena was a *dama* and Delfino a *barelliere*, the names given to female and male volunteers. They'd married in December 1986. Veronica was born the following year, then came the two boys, Pietro and Federico. Aurora came along in 1995.

Lorena was the children's primary caregiver, at least at first. Delfino thought of them as little people without much to say. He had no idea how to change their diapers. Lorena gave them a strong Catholic upbringing. In the mornings, she took them to daycare or to school, where she picked them up in the afternoon for scouts, swimming lessons, soccer, and volleyball, which all took place alongside countless church activities. Lorena cooked the meals and put the kids to sleep after the required evening prayers at the foot of each bed.

Sundays were sacred for her, a day for Mass and church. But Delfino's communion with the Lord was a bit more cavalier. He consecrated his Sundays to soccer. It was his passion and his sickness. He was a member of Mirandola's A. C. Milan club. He and the other members often drove more than two hours from the Bassa to San Siro Stadium, where Baresi, Maldini, Van Basten, and Donadoni dominated Europe for A. C. Milan. Once the children became old enough to understand soccer, Delfino would toss a black-and-red scarf around their necks and take them along. And when he wasn't going to a game, Sunday night was his time to monopolize the remote to the only TV in the house, surfing back and forth between sports and the news. He was well known about town and well liked, but he needed his space.

In 1998, Veronica started sixth grade, Pietro was in fourth grade, Federico was in second, and Aurora had started nursery school. The family lived in a three-bedroom flat on the first floor of an apartment building in the south of Massa, on a small dead-end road.

The police hadn't found anything on the Covezzi-Morselli family. They were irreproachable, as were Giuliano, Lorena's other brothers, and her father, Enzo. But her niece, Cristina, had been crystal clear when she'd named her little cousins. They had been in the cemeteries, she was sure. Social services and police gathered as much information as possible. Occupation, work address, home address. The sting was scheduled for the first light of dawn on Thursday, November 12.

On the morning of Wednesday, November 11, Delfino went to pick up a new Lancia Dedra. The kids were euphoric when he explained to them that it could reach more than 120 mph. That afternoon, they went to eat chestnuts at their grandmother's house. She'd recently been widowed. Lorena wasn't with them. She'd gone to see the Giacco family to find out whether they had any news of their daughter, Margherita. They hadn't seen her in seven months. The whole town had been talking about it. Even though Lorena didn't know them well, she empathized with them because they were going through a similar ordeal as her brother Giuliano was going through.

Oddina Paltrinieri—the neighbor who'd taken Dario in—had spread the rumor that there was something shady about those family separations, but the seed of doubt had already been sown. The Gallieras were considered borderline, the Giaccos were out-of-towners and no one knew them very well, and Giuliano, well, some people thought Giuliano was a bit weird, going around with that weird hair on his head and that wife of his who didn't seem all that normal.

That evening, Lorena put her kids to bed and retired early. The first three were in their room, while Aurora was in a crib in her parents' room. At around five forty a.m., the little one sat up in her crib. "Mommy, pee-pee." Lorena picked her up, brought her to the bathroom and then back to bed. Before returning to her room, she went to the kitchen to pour herself a glass of water. That's when she heard the intercom buzz. Her heart skipped a beat. Who could it be at this hour?

"Ma'am, don't worry. It's the police." Lorena looked out the window and saw some officers in the yard. She counted them as they entered the house. Seven.

"Did something happen to my brother?" she asked.

"No, ma'am," they said. "But please go and wake your husband. We have a warrant to search your home."

Lorena led the officers into the bedroom. They fanned out around the queen bed where Delfino was fast asleep. They woke him up and asked him and Lorena to get dressed. The voices and lights had awoken the children. Lorena could hear them murmuring in their bedroom. The police asked Lorena and Delfino to follow them into the dining room. They'd laid out some papers on the table. Lorena saw some highlighted words: *hoods*, *devils*, *cemeteries*. She didn't understand.

"Your niece made these statements, Mrs. Morselli," explained one of the officers. "Ask your children to get dressed. You're not being investigated, but you have to come with us to the station."

Lorena asked to call her mother, Lina, so she could come watch the kids while she and Delfino went to Mirandola.

"No, ma'am. Your mother can't be here right now. You all have to come with us."

What did they want? Why were they there? The morning sun was starting to light up the house. The officers weren't telling her anything. They opened all her family albums and requested home videos of baptisms, first Communions, and birthdays along with a copy of the weekly magazine *Famiglia Cristiana*, which contained a story on the pedophile case in the Bassa.

The children were allowed to have breakfast, but the police prevented Lorena and Delfino from talking to them. Delfino got straight to the point. "Enough. Let's all go."

When the convoy reached the station, a young woman came to meet them. She smiled and introduced herself as Dr. Donati, a psychologist with AUSL. Lorena and Delfino were asked to go upstairs to sign some papers. Delfino turned to Lorena. "I'll go up—you stay with the kids. Don't leave them alone." Something bad was about to happen. Everyone felt it.

Lorena sat down among her still-sleepy children. Aurora was on her knees, playing with some colored pencils. Veronica, the oldest, started to sob, and Federico followed suit.

"Why are you making them cry?" barked Dr. Donati.

Lorena knew that if she'd snapped back, the situation would have deteriorated. She had to go upstairs, too, but she knew that some time would go by before she'd see her children again. She didn't hug them. She didn't kiss them. She looked at them one last time. Then she turned around and followed Dr. Donati up the stairs.

Up on the second floor, Delfino was sitting between two officers with his head in his hands. He was sobbing. Marcello Burgoni was reading out loud the child protection order from the juvenile court in Bologna. He and Lorena had been neglectful parents. They hadn't looked after their children. They'd left them at the mercy of a band of depraved people. The court was suspending their custodial rights and banning all visits for no less than two months. Crying, Lorena tried to protest. Was this what she got for all her questions over the past few months? When she'd asked about her niece who'd been taken away that summer?

"We're sorry, ma'am."

The children were loaded into squad cars and taken to an unknown location. Confused and dazed, Lorena and Delfino got in their car and sped toward Massa. Lorena wanted to warn her mother immediately. The news would break her heart. After losing Cristina and Riccardo, and now also her grandchildren from Lorena, she was suddenly a grandmother to nobody. When they arrived, they found her in tears.

The police had come at dawn to take everyone away: her husband, Enzo; her eldest son, Emidio; and the youngest, Giuseppe. They arrested Giuliano and Monica at their home in rural Pavignane. Mother and daughter cried for a long time. From one day to the next, an entire family had been wiped away. Lorena did the rounds of her children's schools to talk to their teachers. Had anyone come to talk to the kids lately? The teachers didn't know anything.

When Lorena and Delfino arrived home that evening, they found a devastating silence. Lorena felt like she'd gone back twelve years, to the day she and her husband had returned from their honeymoon. And now here they were, more than a decade later, miserable and exhausted, drying each other's tears while sitting on empty little beds. They cried as they put away toys and looked at the photographs of a happy life that someone had ripped out from under their feet, just like that.

PART III

AN ARMY OF GHOSTS

11.

The old Bellentani meat factory is a complex of buildings as long as a soccer field. It rises along the Provinciale 468, by the southwest entrance to Massa Finalese. It is separated from the two-lane road by a canal. From the '50s until the end of the '70s, it provided jobs for hundreds of men and women. "World-famous deli meats," according to an old midcentury commercial, the one with an African man and a Native American man gulping down prosciuttos hanging from the tree of plenty. Now, it's little more than a mass of crumbling cement. It had been abandoned even before a magnitude 6.1 earthquake caused a piece of the north wall to collapse.

I went in with Alessia one morning in February, bypassing the rusty metal fence erected to keep out local miscreants. The complex was unstable, and another tremor could easily cause the floor to cave in or the roof to collapse. Silence reigned over its spare and spectral halls, interrupted only by the sound of the broken glass and plaster under our feet. Mold and rust had long since taken possession of every corner. We entered right after we'd finished reading a packet of papers at least three fingers thick containing Cristina's statements.

This was the house of horrors she'd built out of LEGO for Dr. Avanzi. This was where she said she'd killed two older children—a ten-year-old boy and a blonde and blue-eyed eight-year-old girl—after the grown-ups had tied them to a table. Giuliano and the "priest" helped her do it. The victims were taken to the old factory from a prison house in the countryside where the blinds were always drawn. Many children lived there, sleeping on the ground like animals and eating leftovers and garbage. Cristina had been there. She'd gone there one evening with her father to bring food to the children. And she'd seen them. Dirty, emaciated, malnourished. They weren't children. They were cattle for the slaughter. Someone told her that they were the Satanists' children. They probably weren't registered and were raised in isolation so they could be abused and sacrificed without anyone noticing their absence.

After being taken to the cemetery and the abandoned meat processing plant, those poor creatures were cut into pieces and hung from hooks in the ceiling. Probably the same ones under which we were walking. We were in a big room on the ground floor, with a white ceiling illuminated by four windows that gave out onto the canal.

In November 1998, Inspector Pagano searched the plant and noticed that just outside it, on the eastern side that bordered the fields, there were a few stables and pigsties. As Pagano approached them, his gaze fell on a few toys that were strewn across the ground, including a tricycle. Next to it was a wooden pole with a "rather showy metal hook" and a trash can full of shoes, "including children's and women's shoes, lying around, scattered all over the place. Then, further on, after the pigsty, was residue from a bonfire, with old ashes from burnt items, and among the burnt things were the remains of a black doll."

Nothing else had been found at the old meat processing plant. No bodies, no trace of human sacrifice, no DNA, no knives, ropes, or tables for altars. Whoever had entered there must have done a fantastic job cleaning up the crime scene and removing any trace of their presence. They'd certainly had the time. Cristina's story had come out four months after she was taken away, and she'd probably been taken to the Bellentani factory even before that, when she was six or seven.

But it was still strange that nobody in town had noticed anything. The Bellentani factory is an imposing structure compared to the other buildings in Massa. And it's only a few feet from a road where cars and trucks drive by at all hours of the day and night. Whoever met there would have had to light up the rooms with multiple flashlights. And lights bouncing off walls and windows in the dark nights of the Bassa would have drawn attention, even from a distance. Plus, the building is surrounded by houses, mostly single-family homes, all within a few hundred feet of it. And yet none of the people questioned by police had ever reported seeing anything strange. Alessia and I found a similar situation at the Massa Finalese cemetery, on the other side of town. We reached it on foot from Bar Pesa, a popular meeting spot at the bend in the road that leads to Mirandola. Even though the cemetery is on a tree-lined street that partially blocks the view from afar, the closest houses are a stone's throw away from the southern wall of the cemetery. Plus, Via Albero is a two-lane road that leads in and out of town. The sidewalk by the cemetery is narrow, and the Devil worshippers would have been forced to form a long line. It seems extremely improbable that dozens of hooded figures with children in tow could have entered without being noticed.

And even if all those children had managed—exhausted from lack of sleep—to climb over the two entrance gates and do all those things—dig up coffins, commit group violence, take part in rituals and sacrifices—cemeteries at night require some kind of illumination. None of Massa's four thousand inhabitants had ever reported seeing the cemetery light up to Mirandola's police or *carabinieri*. And what about the noise? Screams, shrieks, cries of pain. No one had ever heard any of that in the dead of night.

Alessia and I measured the distance from the internal courtyard of the cemetery to the window of the nearest house, on the other side of the parking lot, to be about two hundred feet, more or less the space between the center of a soccer field and the goal. The northern side of the cemetery looked out onto the countryside. But even if the sect had operated in that more isolated area, where the lawn was less crowded with coffins and tombstones, residents of the Palazzina neighborhood, only 260 feet away, would have noticed something. And anyway, thirty people coming and going from such a place late at night, multiple nights a week, can't go completely unnoticed. Especially in a town where rumors abound, and where everyone knows everything about everyone else. After a few days, even I, who'd grown up in Milan, a city of about 1.5 million people, had started to get used to the small-town dynamic. Massa Finalese wasn't much more than a glorified courtyard. Any resident could have spent at least twenty minutes talking to another resident just by listing their relatives, moving on to a chronological and anecdotal recounting of their lives, to finally launch into a string of gossip and sarcastic remarks in dialect (her sister *faceva dei gran buchín*). Whenever I met a parent or relative of one of the removed children, I found that I knew many details about their lives, both true and rumored. Especially the more private ones. No one seemed to have escaped their own community's cruel and systematic scrutiny, or risen above the perverse pleasure of commenting at the misfortune—*disgrassie*—of others.

"That's how it is here," a shopkeeper told me jokingly. "If I close the store for five minutes to go to the bathroom, by the time I open it again, everyone already knows about it."

Could it be that the town's great malicious, prying eye that sees all had missed those bizarre nighttime gatherings?

With three times the residents of Massa Finalese, Finale Emilia feels like a small provincial city. The epicenter of the 2012 earthquake was here, more than three miles under Castello delle Rocche, which partially collapsed and is now propped up by a charmless system of scaffolding. In October 1998, when Cristina started to tell investigators about the rituals in the Massa Finalese cemetery and at the former meat processing plant, Margherita told Dr. Donati what had happened in that castle. Giulio—or Giuly, as she sometimes called the strange character who had molested her in the bar bathroom—took her there with an acquaintance. "There were other children, and they made me go get some of those children myself. They put devil masks on us, and the grown-ups were also wearing devil or vampire masks."

The Satanists used the castle to store the masks and robes they used in the rituals. They made the children get changed there, then they set out in a procession toward the Finale Emilia cemetery. The Castello delle Rocche is in the old town center and is surrounded by dozens of apartment buildings and businesses—bars, shops, pharmacies, restaurants. The neighborhood topography is typical of any old town, with narrow alleys that make it almost impossible for groups of oddly dressed people to pass unnoticed. How would that colorful procession have managed to leave the castle, cross the old center in silence, pass through the Piazza Baccarini roundabout, cross the busy Via Marconi intersection, and turn onto Via Cimitero without being seen?

As in Massa, the Finale Emilia cemetery is on the edge of town. It is also not far from the Panaro River. But it is also surrounded by houses. A pink house is clearly visible from the internal courtyard of the cemetery. Its windows look out onto the expanse of tombstones. A woman named Federica lives there. When we rang her doorbell, she was in the middle of knitting a sweater for her granddaughter. She let us in. The window that looked out on the cemetery was in a bedroom on the second floor. Anyone in that house would have noticed light or noise coming from the cemetery's internal courtyard. But Federica, who'd lived there since before the pedophile case erupted, had never noticed anything. She also hadn't been questioned by the police.

"This is the first anyone's asked me anything," she said, perplexed. "Are you sure the children were talking about this cemetery?"

I couldn't believe it. If anyone in that area might have seen something happen there at night, it would have been her. Why hadn't anyone taken the time to knock on her door? Hadn't Margherita identified the area as the sect's epicenter? When she went there with Dr. Donati and investigators, she'd pointed to the precise spots she remembered being taken to by Santo and the Satanists.

The cemetery custodian, Filippo Neri, who lived next to the tombs, told police that he'd never seen anything. Not the large piles of earth that would have been there the following morning had someone dug any holes or burrowed six feet into a grave or dug up plots for new corpses. Nothing at all. As if whoever went there at night to dig and churn up earth, and to slit human and animal throats, had left everything just as it was before.

"There was a blade that fell from above and cut people," Margherita said. "One time, a boy's head fell on me, and I was very scared. They put the heads and other parts in a basket and threw them in the river."

The Panaro River flows just six hundred feet from the cemetery. That was where, one Saturday three years before, in 1995, five boys from Finale Emilia had chanced upon a skull while fishing. That skull had meant nothing to the district attorney at the time, but somebody remembered it, and they were going to use it to help connect the dots in this horror story. The medical examiner's phone rang again. He headed to the archives to fish out the strange skull with no jaw or organic residue, which had mystified Dr. Beduschi and his colleagues.

But something still didn't make sense. According to Margherita, the Satanists didn't throw the body parts into the section of the Panaro that runs by the Finale Emilia cemetery where the skull was found. They threw them somewhere else entirely, in a town called Casoni, about twenty miles from Finale Emilia. Why go all that way when they could have just turned away from the tombstones, crossed the short tract of uninhabited land by the riverbank, and entered the only blind spot available, far from homes, roads, and prying eyes? There, in the dark, under the cover of trees and fog, it wouldn't have been that difficult to get rid of a body. Why drive all the way to Casoni? Margherita knew the area. Before moving to Massa Finalese, the Giaccos had lived there for a few years, and Flora, one of Margherita's older sisters, was still there. But Inspector Pagano hadn't discovered anything in Casoni or the surrounding area, other than the fact that Flora's house was very close to the riverbank "and that a few feet away, there's a little path that leads to the riverbank," from where "one could dispose of anything in no time." But the prosecution didn't want to leave any stone unturned. To try to find the bodies, they hired a company to dredge up the Panaro and to sound out its depths with mobile flotation devices. The operation cost 150,000,000 lira ($88,000). Nothing was found.

Despite long and expensive investigations across the territory and home searches of suspects, no evidence was turned up, at least nothing that seemed relevant to the case. A few pornographic magazines and videos, a pair of boots with heels, an old Polaroid, but never a weapon or a trace of blood or photos or videos that showed acts of pedophilia or snuff films set in cemeteries.

After the dawn blitz on November 12, 1998, Lorena's children were each placed with a different family. They were assigned a schedule of visits with Dr. Donati at her office at the Cenacolo Francescano in Reggio Emilia. Dr. Donati used the space to meet with the children who had been removed. She'd gotten to know the nuns well, and the building they managed was convenient for the foster families, all of whom lived in the area. It was also far enough from Mirandola that the children didn't risk running into a parent or other family member.

The Covezzis hadn't said anything all winter, but after two months, social services extended the suspension of their custody, keeping Lorena and her husband from having any contact whatsoever with their children. The Covezzis didn't keep quiet after that. They immediately mobilized lawyers and journalists, gave interviews, and participated in TV programs. The Honorable Carlo Giovanardi took an interest in their story, and in March 1999, along with lawyer and senator Augusto

Cortelloni, he brought the case to Justice Minister Oliviero Diliberto through a parliamentary interrogation. The document was long and detailed and ended with a question: "Why did they take away children who'd never said anything, and above all, children whose parents aren't even under investigation?"

But on March 17, the day before the minister was scheduled to respond, the Covezzis received an arrest warrant. After four months, their two oldest children, Veronica and Pietro, had accused them of sexual abuse. What a strange coincidence. Veronica said Delfino abused her while Lorena spied on them from behind the door. She said that her maternal uncles, whom her cousin Cristina had also accused, were monsters. They blindfolded her in a barn and took turns abusing her with a "metal bar." Pietro, the second child, spoke right after Veronica. Their uncle Giuseppe, their mother's musician brother, sodomized him "with an awl." Uncle Emidio did the same thing with sandpaper. The abuses occurred at home and in the chicken coop of their maternal grandparents' home, where Uncle Giuliano whipped him and his siblings with electric wires. Federico was the third to speak up. Aurora, who was only three, provided just a few flashes of memories of her mother leaving the keys attached to the door so some "Moroccans" could come into the house whenever they wanted to.

The children never saw each other during this time or talked to each other or were given the chance to influence each other. But they each explained to Dr. Donati what happened when they were taken to the cemeteries. "They tied us to a wooden cross, then they started throwing daggers at us, knives . . . They made us hold a really hot horseshoe in our hands . . . These priests here sharpened the knives, then sometimes they threw them at us . . . They made us burn some Jesus crosses, because they didn't believe in Jesus. I mean, they believed in the Devil, because the Devil does bad things, and they wanted to do bad things, too. Then, when they set fire to the crosses, they made us pray to the Devil . . . They tied us up and surrounded us with firecrackers and lit them . . . They hurt us in our bottoms with a nail file, an awl, pliers, sandpaper . . . They took us there in our underwear, even though it was the middle of winter, even in the snow . . . Then, one time, there were children in the van, and they put two big mice in there . . ." Pietro gave investigators the most disturbing details of all: he said his parents helped him kill a lot of children in a parish theater. At least fifteen children per week.

The Covezzi children, it seemed, saw their parents as depraved, bloodthirsty people. Certainly not as devotees of the Madonna of Lourdes. And certainly not as model and pious parents. It didn't matter that their religious community had rallied around Lorena and Delfino in solidarity. The children didn't want to go back home. In fact, their foster families were surprised by how little they'd cried for Mommy and Daddy, and by how quickly they'd adjusted and grown attached to their new parents.

Part of me was still baffled by the actual dynamics of these events, while another part of me couldn't understand why the Covezzi children would *also* be making such serious accusations against their parents. Veronica was twelve years old. She wasn't a little girl anymore. She was almost a teenager. She was much more developed and more aware of the world around her than a seven-year-old child like Dario or an eight-year-old girl like Marta would be. Why would she lie? Why make such brutal allegations against the people who, in theory, she loved more than anyone else in the world? I couldn't explain it. Not as a journalist and not as a father of two young children who'd transformed my whole existence. This story was like a black hole. The more I looked into it, the more it seemed to bend social and behavioral norms and alter the relationship between cause and effect—things I'd always taken for granted. It seemed like a parallel universe where everything was deformed. It terrified me, but I felt its perverse attraction. I couldn't pull away. It became an obsession. I didn't read about anything else. I didn't talk about anything else. Nothing else interested me. At dinner with friends, at work, wherever I was, I inevitably turned the conversation to this. Everyone I talked to would end up staring at me with fear and bewilderment. And the more I probed, the more I sensed danger. I'd never worked on anything like this. It was made of something murky, sticky, and dark, and it stuck to me long after I put away my folders and my notes.

I felt uncomfortable and deeply confused. Over the years, I'd built armor around myself to avoid being affected by the suffering of others. Now, for the first time, I was forced to confront anxieties and fears able to pierce that armor. These children—whose tragedies had become my daily bread—were about the same ages as my children. What had they seen or experienced at home? Could it be true, as their parents believed, that someone had conditioned them? And if it was possible to do that, can a stranger really destroy, so quickly, the deep love that binds mother and child? I was afraid of the little things, the daily gestures. Afraid that my children would see me walking around naked after a shower and maybe say something or draw something at daycare that someone might misunderstand. Afraid that even a simple act, like giving them a bath, could one day turn against me if someone just asked them, "Have your parents ever touched you?" But it couldn't be that simple. There had to be something else happening to those families in Massa and Mirandola that I didn't know about. I pored over hundreds of pages day and night, without being able to clear the fog that seemed to envelop every line. How much of it was true? All of it? It couldn't be. Nothing? It didn't make sense. Where was the line between real and imagined? Who had drawn it and how? There was no way to find out.

12.

Alessia and I spent months poring over documents. We reconstructed the entire case. Five trials, about twenty suspects, convictions, and acquittals that alternated and overlapped, sometimes creating the impression that there was no logic to what had happened.

When this story broke in 1997, it set off legal proceedings that initially concerned a very small group of people, known as the Pedophiles-1. They included the Gallieras, Federico Scotta, Rosa, and Fredone. At the time, they were charged with sexual abuse against Dario, Marta, Elisa, and Nick at home and in unidentified apartments in the area. All suspects were convicted at the criminal trial in Modena, at the Appeals Court in Bologna, and at the Cassation Court in Rome.

While the Pedophiles-1 trial was in progress, in October 1999, the children who were involved from the start made additional revelations. The newly removed children also provided some new information, which launched a parallel trial called Pedophiles-2. This involved the suspects from the first case, plus the new ones Margherita, Cristina, and the four Covezzi children had accused: Don Giorgio Govoni, Santo Giacco and his son Antonio, and Giuliano, Monica, and the whole Morselli family, along with a mother from Mirandola and a father from Massa Finalese. The suspects in Pedophiles-1 had been charged with domestic sexual acts against minors aged zero to eleven. In Pedophiles-2, they were also charged with holding meetings of an orgiastic and ritualistic nature in cemeteries. Don Giorgio and Rita Spinardi, Dario's teacher in Pegognaga, were accused of working together to deprive Dario of his personal freedom and to take him out of school to threaten him.

More than a year after their removals, the children didn't seem to want to see their families again. In October 1998, when Cristina had been living with her foster family for only three months, she wrote a two-page letter to the judges working on her case. I found it among the hundreds of pages of documents and statements in Don Ettore's archives. From her new bedroom at her new family house, Cristina wanted to vent her rage and claim her right to be heard and believed.

> Dear Judge,
>
> Put these people on trial, but there's one thing I really don't now [sic] those other people I told Emma [Avanzi] about from the group of those men that I don't now [sic] the name, and I don't remember them. I will tri [sic] at all costs to make myself remember who those people were I think they were people who now [sic] my parents and maybe they are also friends with my parents. The head of the group maybe is a priest who was studying the life of Jesus and of God. Judge, I believe in God, Mary, Jesus and I now [sic] they will love me like parents . . . I'm very unhappy and it will take some time to make me understand the things that happened. I will tri [sic] very hard to try to understand. But first I want to tell you: if my parents and uncles start to say that the things I say are true, be a little bit nice to them, but until they tell the truth, always stay harsh.

The court asked medical consultants from Centro Studi Hansel e Gretel (the Hansel and Gretel Research Center) in Turin—an organization leading the fight against pedophilia—to perform psychodiagnostic examinations on the children. Psychologists Cristina Roccia, Sabrina Farci, and Alessandra Pagliuca listened to the children and recorded videos of their meetings alone or with the judges. They "absolutely ruled out the presence of mental pathologies that could invalidate their ability to distinguish fantasy from reality," or to cause the children "to invent accusations." Their personality profiles were "typical of victims, fully compatible with having experienced violence." The psychologists determined that in all cases, the children's testimonies were initially fragmented, exhibiting the so-called "cluster sampling that consists of an initially threadbare account, with an increasing amount of new details emerging over time." The children showed a psychological progression containing "coherent logic typical of traumatized victims," where revelations become increasingly serious as the children overcome their self-imposed silence caused by trauma, fear, and lingering familial affections. In his indictment, prosecutor Claudiani listed the proof he intended to use to corner the suspects: the statements the children had made first to Dr. Donati and her colleagues in Mirandola, then to the consultants from Turin; Dr. Maggioni's medical results; the various fragments of evidence that Inspector Pagano had gathered during his searches, including vaginal suppositories found at the Morselli home, which Cristina had mentioned when talking about her abuses; and the transcript of a phone conversation overheard in prison, where Monica referred to Don Giorgio Govoni as the "antichrist." Then there was the missing page from Dario's planner, which allegedly contained drawings of Giorgios One and Two, along with the confirmation that the priest drove a white van—the same one other children said they'd seen him load with dead bodies after the sacrifices. There was also the skull found in the Panaro River in 1995, which Claudiani wanted to use to "demonstrate a pattern of disposal of human remains, including of the ones that were exhumed in the area." That bone was proof that something had happened in these cemeteries, proof that the children weren't lying. Still, there was no evidence of the dozens of murders mentioned in the evidentiary hearings. Having found nothing among missing person reports from the years of the crimes, investigators reasoned that the sacrificial victims must have come from somewhere else. Probably Eastern Europe. In fact, Dario had said he'd killed an Albanian child and seen the body being burned in the fireplace. The war in Kosovo had recently ended, causing refugees to flow into Albania and Western Europe. And the previous conflict, which had split up Yugoslavia, had transformed the Balkans into a hotbed of human trafficking, especially of women, but also of children, according to some reports. For example, Inspector Pagano and his team had found a woman in her fifties who had left her native Bosnia with her son and lived in Finale Emilia, where "she did cleaning work in churches." But then they discovered that she'd run away from an abusive husband and was not involved in human trafficking. Charges of ritual killings were immediately dropped due to a total absence of proof.

But the atmosphere that prevailed in the courtroom—which I pieced together with court transcripts—remained extremely hostile. On the opening day of the Pedophiles-2 trial, one of the lawyers for Dr. Donati and Dr. Burgoni's organization took the stand and turned to the Morselli and Covezzi families with hate in his eyes. "We're here to ask you to pay for the pain you inflicted on those who today have become the children of the AUSL, the ones who used to be your children and who are no longer yours. They're our children now, and we will stand up for them in every way!"

At the trial, technical consultants for the court, the defense, and the prosecution—including Dr. Donati—took turns on the stand, often giving very different interpretations of the evidence. The lawyers and expert witnesses for the defense objected to the methods used by the Mirandola social workers. They alleged conditioning of the witnesses and latticed allegations, due to their often overlapping nature. They accused the psychologists of posing clearly leading questions designed to get the children to confirm preestablished and baseless theories, which the experts had developed despite not having any experience in such cases, by their own admission.

The judges believed the children were credible. End of story. And not just because of Dr. Donati, but also because of the experts from Turin, who weren't connected to her. The court supported the prosecution's thesis and defended Dr. Donati's actions. As they specified in their verdict, to do otherwise, "one would have to conclude that the psychologist . . . had knowingly violated every basic rule of her training," with the aim of leading the children to make up plausible stories "fully knowing the damage she'd inflict upon children and adults. Why would she do such a thing?"

Dr. Maggioni's medical examinations had found signs of abuse—extremely serious abuse—in all the children. The evidence stood up in court, despite the fact that the forensic examiners and gynecologists who analyzed her pictures of the children's genitals—which were projected onto a large screen in court—didn't think these signs were all that obvious.

One of the most heated moments of the trial came during the debate between Dr. Maggioni, consulting for the prosecution, and Cristina Cattaneo, an anatomical pathologist from Milan who consulted for the defense during the evidentiary hearings. According to Dr. Cattaneo, Lorena and Delfino's children showed no signs that "clearly demonstrated acts of sexual abuse." When Dr. Maggioni pointed to a photo of a girl's genitals and said her hymen seemed to have disappeared due to repetitive and serious acts of violence, Dr. Cattaneo pointed out that the hymen was actually clearly visible.

During the ensuing debate, Dr. Maggioni said that after the arrival of menarche—the first menstrual cycle—a torn hymen can grow back. Her colleagues flinched. The claim has no scientific basis. The defense reared up. It began questioning Dr. Maggioni's competence. She was the one who'd examined all the children. Her reports were instrumental in their removal from their families. And many defense consultants disagreed with Dr. Maggioni's conclusions, including Antonio Fornari, a forensic medicine superstar from Pavia. He'd handled some very famous cases in his career. Upon analyzing Dr. Maggioni's work and methods, he said, "I absolutely disagree . . . I don't see anything at all that could indicate, with any degree of certainty, that these children have undergone sexual abuse."

The court formed a panel of experts to put the disagreement to rest. The panel established a profile of "suspected" or "indicative" instances of abuse for some of the children and determined that some of the marks in the genital regions—rhagades, little incisions, redness—could be interpreted either as common lesions or physical traits, or as traces "compatible" with acts of violence. But there was no certainty. None of the children showed "specific" or "definite" signs. In fact—as modern scientific textbooks on the subject explain—it's only possible to be absolutely certain sexual violence was inflicted on a minor when there are unequivocal traces like lacerations, pregnancies, or sexually transmitted diseases. But the weight of the children's accusations against their parents more than made up for this forensic uncertainty. In May 2000, the prosecution in the Pedophiles-2 trial asked for sentences of up to fifteen years in prison, including for Don Giorgio Govoni, who was considered one of the leaders of the sect.

Some of the don's old flock and friends told me that he seemed calm and resigned to his fate, even after his involvement became known all across the Bassa. He only trusted *giustissia divina*, divine justice. He'd seen the human kind flounder in the courtrooms, hearing after hearing, testimony after testimony. On the afternoon of May 19, Don Giorgio got in his car and left Staggia for Modena to see his lawyer, Pier Francesco Rossi. He didn't have an appointment. The priest, as usual, had alerted Rossi of his arrival with a quick call. He had to give him "something important."

Rossi was with a client that day but said he'd find a minute for him. He was a young criminal lawyer and a rising star on Modena's legal scene. He'd met Don Giorgio three years before, when he was assigned to represent Dario's older brother, Igor Galliera, after he was accused of molesting and abusing the boy. At the time, Igor was twenty-two years old but incapable of finding his lawyer's office on his own. Instead of arriving by bus from Massa Finalese, he'd asked Don Giorgio to drive him there. When the don ended up among the suspects, he chose the same defense lawyer.

Don Giorgio sat down in the waiting room. Then, from inside his office, Rossi heard someone wheezing. Someone knocked on his door and yelled, "Don Giorgio's not feeling well!" The priest was lying facedown on the floor, his body gripped by spasms. Rossi rushed over to him. Even the arrival of an ambulance didn't do anything to help. Don Giorgio died in his lawyer's arms, felled by a heart attack.

News of Don Giorgio's death traveled across the Bassa in just a few hours. At dusk, all the bells sounded the death knell, the soundtrack to four funerals held in the places where he'd lived and where he'd spread the Gospel through sweat and sacrifice. It was the lament of the thousands of churchgoers who'd been by his side since the very beginning. They wanted their anger to be heard all the way in the courtrooms of Modena. Someone in the night had vandalized the mourning posters in San Felice with the words *pig* and *bastard* a few hours after Don Giorgio's death. But in San Biagio, Massa, Finale Emilia, and Staggia, Don Giorgio had already become a martyr. He was the latest victim of a monster that was leaving a trail of bodies and suffering families in its wake. National papers caught wind of the story, while the local press filled their headlines with quotes from relatives, acquaintances, and church members: "Those judges shouldn't quit their day jobs." "They're the ones that killed him." "The police just wanted to frame him." "Let's march against the prosecutors." "Satan is deceiving their minds."

A few days later, Pedophiles-2 closed with a slew of extremely harsh sentences. Thirteen defendants were convicted, including the Gallieras and Federico, who'd already been convicted in Pedophiles-1, along with Santo Giacco, the entire Morselli family, and Rita Spinardi. The court decided not to rule on Don Giorgio due to "the death of the guilty."

Rita Spinardi paid one of the steepest prices in that round of convictions before they were even handed down. Two years before, the ministry of education had suspended her from teaching. Alone, with no children, and still on the mend after a complicated surgery, she'd started delivering phone books door-to-door or working in bars to supplement her 700,000 lira ($450) per month welfare checks, which were just enough to cover rent and legal fees. When she wasn't working, she volunteered at the Mantova Caritas, where she prepared meals at a center for vulnerable people. She spent the rest of her time at home, blinds drawn to protect herself from the paranoia that was overwhelming her, sometimes in the form of an old, green Fiat 124 that seemed to follow her everywhere. Was it real? Or a vision cast by the shock and fear of recent events? Her phone was tapped, and her life had ended up in the pages of the *Gazzetta di Mantova*, which had implied she'd helped kidnap that poor little boy from Gonzaga. The prosecution had accused her of hiding the drawings Dario had made of Giorgios One and Two in his planner, effectively tampering with evidence. The defense maintained that these two strange characters hadn't come to persecute Dario from Massa Finalese, but from a dark, remote corner of his mind created by the trauma caused by hours and hours of questions posed by an anxious foster mother and a young, inexperienced psychologist.

A year later, during her darkest days, Rita was acquitted by a court in Bologna. The Court of Appeals dropped all charges of abuse in cemeteries for lack of proof, partially reversing the Modena court's verdicts. Santo Giacco and two other parents were also acquitted, while the convictions for domestic abuse were confirmed for Enzo, Emidio, Giuliano, Monica, and Giuseppe Morselli. The Court of Cassation in 2002 confirmed the verdict by the Court of Appeals. It became increasingly clear to the public that something had gone wrong in the trials of the Devils of the Bassa.

Yet that same year, another lawsuit began. Pedophiles-3 only involved Lorena and Delfino, who were charged with abusing their children. The Covezzis hadn't heard from them in more than three years. Lorena had been living abroad for just as long. In 1999, as her children started to confirm Cristina's stories to Dr. Donati and their foster parents, Lorena found out that she was pregnant with her fifth child. Even though she had turned to her almighty God every night since learning to pray, he hadn't defended her family from being dismantled and thrown into jail. But now, it was as if he were allowing her one last grip on her sanity before she slid into an abyss without return. For months, she told no one, hiding her secret under increasingly loose clothing. Her lawyers warned her. It wasn't a good idea to give birth in Mirandola. The year before, on July 17, 1998, Kaempet and Federico had had their third child, Stella. But as Kaempet was being sewn up in the operating room after a Cesarean, social services arrived with a ruling from the juvenile court and moved the newborn to a room that was inaccessible to her parents. Then they took the baby to a foster home and erased all trace of her.

"If you stay here, they'll do the same to you," the lawyers told Lorena and Delfino. Lorena was worried. She turned to her church and volunteer communities.

"There are some French priests in Finale Emilia," Don Ettore Rovatti told her. "Let me ask what they can do."

The Saint-Jean brothers were the guardians of the Sanctuary of the Obici. They had contacts in Salernes, in the south of France, where they knew people who ran a foster home that could help the Covezzis hide the newborn. Lorena and Delfino left their town one night in December 1999 on an almost seven-hour drive into the unknown. Their son was born on December 27. They named him Stefano. Lorena stayed with him in Salernes, while Delfino traveled back and forth to the Bassa to work and to keep a close eye on their legal troubles.

The trial took a bad turn for them right at the very beginning. Soon after Lorena's escape to France, one of the children accused her lawyer of intimidating him during a detention hearing and telling him that Dr. Donati would be "dead by the time she was fifty." The lawyer was indicted and forced to resign from the defense team. When I met up with him in his office years later, he told me that his wife had begged him to quit the case, fearing that someone would take away their young daughter.

The Covezzis had to find a new lawyer, but that wasn't the end of their troubles. The children continued to accuse them of pressuring and threatening them. Two of them told Dr. Donati, around the same time, that Lorena had approached them as they left their new schools. "I'm telling you—don't tell them things, or we'll kill you!" she'd supposedly said. Lorena started keeping a detailed diary with all her daily movements, marking down the names of people in France who could say they'd seen her. She held on to receipts from meals, highway tolls, and rest stops, as well as her home phone records.

She went to Italy as little as possible. She started looking for a new job in Salernes. Nothing to do with daycare or children, or with anything she'd ever studied or learned about in the past twenty years. She would have settled for a job as a *femme de ménage*, a cleaning lady. She was terrified by the idea that someone could find Stefano in France and take him away while she was in Italy.

Initially, Lorena and Delfino were convicted and sentenced to twelve years in prison. Then they were acquitted. The Court of Cassation made them repeat the appeal, but they were judged innocent again. Delfino died of a heart attack in 2013, before learning the outcome of the last verdict, which came in 2014. During the second appeal, the Court of Cassation had expressed doubts about the methods used by the Mirandola psychologists and the technical consultants from Turin. It held that the children's stories "lacked confirmation of any form and were received in a credulous manner" by the doctors. These same psychologists, whom Modena's court had appreciated for their competence a year before, during the Pedophiles-1 and Pedophiles-2 trials, were now being called "young and lacking in specialized experience." The Court of Cassation specifically pointed out how incredible it was that such a complex and delicate case had been given to them, of all people. It also said it was shocked by how "after the medical examination, the psychologists told the children that the doctors thought someone had really hurt them," especially since it was later determined that those examinations were full of mistakes. Lorena was acquitted "for not having committed the deed." Sixteen years after her children—now adults, now far away, now bitterly angry with her—were taken away in the dead of night.

Meanwhile, Monica, Cristina's mother and Lorena's sister-in-law, had died in a Modena prison after a sharp decline in physical and psychological health. A series of epileptic fits, which had started a few months after her arrest, had worn her out. She stopped being able to write, she had trouble talking and walking, and in her last meeting with Giuliano, who was housed in the same prison as she was, two police officers had needed to hold her up by the arms. She was felled by cerebral thrombosis while in her cell. Enzo, the Morselli family patriarch, soon followed after complications from a stroke, three days after swearing to his wife, Lina, in front of a crucifix, that he'd never touched his granddaughters and grandsons.

Lorena's brothers' problems continued beyond the Pedophiles-2 trial. They were brought into a new criminal trial in which they were the only defendants. Pedophiles-4 took place in Reggio Emilia. Veronica, the eldest child, had told Dr. Donati that she'd been approached by her grandfather and her uncles Emidio and Giuseppe as she left her new school. They kidnapped her a total of four times, each time just before she could board her school bus. They then took her to a nearby woods and raped her with a tree branch. None of the dozens of school children around saw anything. After the rapes, her relatives would leave her somewhere near her foster parents' home before vanishing. Despite the extreme seriousness of the injuries Veronica described, the Reggio Emilia court never authorized a medical examination. After more than ten years, Pedophiles-4 ended in acquittals for all defendants. The prosecutor, who hadn't believed Veronica's accounts, told me that immediately after the verdict, someone from the Modena district attorney's office called him to complain and ask why he'd chosen a different direction from the one taken by his Modenese colleagues up to that point. Even the fifth and last trial, where the Covezzis' former lawyer was charged with intimidating the children, had ended with a conviction in Modena, which was followed by an acquittal on appeal.

In hindsight, the entire legal matter looked like a big, abandoned city planned by an architect who had gone mad along the way. Nothing followed any recognizable logic: two-way roads with no outlet; overpasses over nothing; curved, Escher-like buildings where each floor, each staircase, and each wall obeyed to its own law of gravity. The children's accusations were deemed credible when they were made toward some of the suspects but not toward others. As if the judges had been cherry-picking evidence, giving credence to some segments of testimony while overlooking others. From any angle you looked at it, this story was incredibly grotesque. The defendants had been convicted and acquitted based on the same evidence.

I often thought back to Don Ettore Rovatti's archives, and to the first time I found myself looking at all his folders. Pounds upon pounds of paper that could have easily touched the ceiling when stacked. Hearing transcripts, defense memos, expert witness reports, transcriptions, and interrogations. It was hard to determine the exact number of people who'd worked on the case over almost twenty years. Lawyers, judges, police officers, psychologists, psychiatrists, gynecologists, forensic scientists, and professors from all across Italy. Not to mention the dozens of witnesses and experts called in to give depositions. How many thousands of hours of work had they put in? How much had it cost? Five trials seemed to have done everything except answer the key question: Had those children been abused or not?

Alessia and I tried to make sense of our folders, asking ourselves how likely it was that so many experts from different schools and specializations had managed to make such questionable choices in the same case.

One of the pillars on which the prosecution had built its case was Dr. Maggioni's medical reports. Could they really all be wrong? Could a doctor from a renowned clinic like the Mangiagalli Center be so wrong, so many times?

Maybe.

Our suspicions were sparked by a case in Milan, where Dr. Maggioni worked. While the trials continued in Modena, where she was the star of the show as a consultant for the prosecution, Dr. Maggioni had landed in a ferocious controversy on another abuse case, this time in a court in Milan. The case did not achieve the same notoriety as the one from the Bassa Modenese, but it ruined her career and greatly undermined her credibility. The case involved Marino Viola, a taxi driver accused of sexually abusing his three-year-old daughter.

In 1996, Viola's wife noticed that their little girl had started to use the word *pisello* ("penis") a lot, especially when talking about her father. She and her husband turned to Centro per il Bambino Maltrattato (CBM), the Center for Abused Children, in Milan, an institute that is well known among professionals who deal with minors. A psychologist from the center immediately warned Viola's wife that this was a case of sexual abuse, probably by the father. The woman needed to leave her husband right away and move the girl to a protected location, otherwise she'd be considered an accomplice and risk losing her daughter. The woman knew her husband was innocent, but she panicked and followed the psychologist's instructions. Pietro Forno took up the case. He was a famous prosecutor known for chasing down suspected pedophiles. He relied on a coterie of experts who helped him find cases of abuse and drag the perpetrators to court.

Forno's most trusted consultants included CBM psychologists and Dr. Maggioni. But three years after the trial began, Forno was replaced by another prosecutor, Tiziana Siciliano. After studying the case, she asked for Mr. Viola's acquittal. She then gave Dr. Maggioni a serious dressing down. "I will never give you a consultancy," Siciliano said in her reprimand. "Let's just say that you don't seem to know a whole lot about the subject," she wrote. She also stated that "an extremely wide body of photographic documentation contradicts Dr. Maggioni's declarations so completely that one wonders whether she is utterly incompetent or if she actually means harm . . . I think these are false reports.

The conversation with Dr. Maggioni took a strange turn. I had trouble following her. She responded to my insistent questions with other questions. "What do you want me to do? Do you want me to stop being a doctor for the rest of my days?"

By now, I'd developed a pretty clear idea of the enormous legal mess that this case had become—and of the weakness of the medical evidence that had randomly convicted some and acquitted others. But there was still a big mystery lurking behind this story: the children's accounts. I didn't understand their origins. I didn't understand how such small children had been able to verbalize such horrors. Elements of fantasy were very likely involved. But I had doubts. What if something really had happened in their homes? I would only find the answer far from Mirandola and Massa Finalese, on another continent, in another time.

13.

The last thing that Bridget Bishop saw before closing her eyes forever was the small crowd that had gathered on Gallows Hill on a late-spring day in 1692. It was where alleged witches were hanged, and that was where Bishop ended up, her hands tied behind her back, after a Salem judge condemned her to death. Twice married, in her sixties, and with a combative personality and a flamboyant style, Bishop stood out sharply in a community of mostly Puritan Protestants. She was accused of using witchcraft to curse several girls that had been showing signs of illness and throwing hysterical fits.

The girls' conditions were initially blamed on three women, including a homeless woman and a Caribbean slave who confessed under threat and named three others, including Bishop.

Witnesses claimed that Bishop ran a disreputable establishment for local youths, where some strange things happened. When she appeared before the judges, some of the girls identified her as a witch. Upon seeing her, they started screaming and reported feeling pain. For the judges, this was irrefutable proof of Bishop's guilt—spectral evidence didn't lie. Bishop was sentenced to death, and on June 10, the hangman fit her neck with a rope. She was the first in a long line of accused witches to be targeted by her community. Another eighteen hangings would follow, along with a death by pressing, before the local government put an end to the persecution and some of the girls, now adults, retracted their accusations.

Ancient and contemporary history everywhere in the world abounds with witch hunts like the one in Salem at the end of the seventeenth century. Previously, European Jews were a frequent target and were often accused of conducting violent rituals and child sacrifice. For generations, many Christians believed that Jews used the blood of Christian children to prepare their traditional unleavened bread. One of the first written accounts occurred in Norwich, England, in 1144. That year, the city of East Anglia was shocked by the mysterious murder of a twelve-year-old tanner's apprentice named William. His death was blamed on members of the Jewish community. Similar events appear in annals and news reports from all over the world. They're all born of a similar root: the idea, or the fear, that in every community there are individuals or groups of people leading double lives, lacking all sense of good, who are ready to commit atrocities in the name of absolute evil. Hooded men and women who operate in the dark. Animal sacrifices, especially of cats. Blood-drinking rituals. Black Masses in cemeteries featuring the exhumation of corpses. Sexual violence. Murder. Cannibalism. The same elements that recur in medieval accounts show up in popular movies and TV shows today. Satanism is always there, the eternal anti-Christian threat that celebrates the angel who defied God in the Apocalypse.

Before I started covering the case of the Devils of the Bassa, my knowledge of Satanism was limited to a few articles I'd read, novels and movies I'd consumed, and urban legends I'd heard in childhood. Then I came across a text by an academic in Turin, Massimo Introvigne. In *Satanism: A Social History*, he explains that this phenomenon has fairly recent origins. The first Satanists known to history appeared in France, between the seventeenth and eighteenth centuries. A courtesan at Louis

XIV's court, Catherine La Voisin, was caught organizing the first Black Masses, rituals in which she and other court dames worshipped the Devil in exchange for favors or material gain. A century later, Aleister Crowley, an English student of the occult, defined the basic rules of Satanism: "'Do what thou wilt' shall be the whole of the Law. There is no god but Man." These rules laid the foundations for the Thelema Abbey, which he built at the start of the 1920s in Cefalú, near Palermo. The local papers reported that Crowley held sex parties that included sodomy and animal sacrifices. They started calling him "the king of depravity, the wickedest man in the world, the great beast," leading Benito Mussolini's government to expel him from the country.

Satanism first came into the light in 1966, when esoterist Anton LaVey founded the Church of Satan in California, turning the movement into a full-blown religion. To this day, it has a registered office, a website, and a radio station. Adherents worship Lucifer not so much as evil incarnate, but as a symbol of freedom, which they associate with pleasures like power, sex, and money.

Until the end of the 1960s, the US media wasn't very interested in sects and ritual killings. Then, in August 1969, Charles Manson's followers stabbed Sharon Tate and four other people to death at her home in Los Angeles. The ritual killings shocked the nation, and people quickly pointed to Manson as the Devil incarnate. In the 1970s, writers like Stephen King started to popularize the horror genre. Films like *The Exorcist*, which came out in 1973, did their part to captivate the public, while at the same time making it confront its deepest fears and anxieties.

Nine years after the Manson Family massacred Sharon Tate and her friends, the mass suicide of more than nine hundred followers of Reverend Jim Jones shocked America. Jones convinced dozens of families to follow him to a village in Guyana, where they lived in an agricultural community founded on principles of apostolic socialism, an ideology strong on conspiracy theories. Relatives of some of the followers became worried and turned to Leo Ryan, a politician from

California. He flew to the Amazon with a delegation of journalists to visit the area, but some of Jones's followers opened fire, killing Ryan and four other people. That same evening, Jones convinced his people that the Army was coming for them. He handed out punch laced with cyanide and filmed his last sermon amidst the agonizing cries of men, women, and children. A third of the victims were children. They were found, days later, piled up in the temple. News of Jonestown's "revolutionary suicide" made the biggest headlines of the year, sparking a new wave of panic. These sects seemed able to manipulate peoples' minds and lead normal individuals to inconceivable collective actions.

Two years later, in 1980, American stores started selling the book that would unleash the Satanic Panic, one of the biggest cases of mass hysteria of all time. *Michelle Remembers* was the story of Michelle Smith, a twenty-seven-year-old woman from Victoria, British Columbia, who had sought treatment for depression from Dr. Lawrence Pazder. After their first meeting, Dr. Pazder realized that, although she had no memory of it, Michelle's depression was the result of abuse she'd suffered as a child. He decided to use hypnosis to bring her repressed memories back to the surface. One day, Michelle jolted awake after dreaming that hundreds of tiny spiders were coming out of a cut in her left arm. Soon after, she started remembering a long string of abusive episodes she'd experienced when she was five years old. A satanic group had forced her into orgies, rituals, sacrifices, torture, and rapes. She said she was locked in a cage during the rituals. The Satanists covered her in the blood of the children and adults they'd killed and tied her to a corpse inside a car that then crashed into the side of the road.

The book was an instant sensation, selling an astronomical number of copies in America. Dozens of papers and TV programs started to cover stories of people who said they'd lived similar experiences or who reported murders committed by a presumed satanic group. Some papers expressed doubts about the veracity of Michelle's accounts, but by then, her story had shaken millions of Americans. There was a new enemy in town—internal, invisible, and far more dangerous than the Communist menace represented by the distant Soviet Union. This one could worm its way into cities and schools, where it attacked the smallest and most helpless members of society. And it had a name: SRA, which stood for "satanic ritual abuse."

Three years after *Michelle Remembers* came out, a mother in Manhattan Beach, California, noticed that her two-and-a-half-year-old son was behaving strangely. After peppering him with questions, she decided he'd been abused by the McMartins, the family that ran his preschool. The woman, who was later diagnosed with psychosis, reported some very strange stories to the police. Her son had allegedly seen his teachers have sex with animals during class, and one day, he'd seen his teacher, Ray Buckey, fly.

The police sent a letter to about two hundred parents of children who were currently attending the preschool or who had gone there in the past:

> Dear parent,
>
> This Department is conducting a criminal investigation involving child molestation . . . We are asking your assistance in this continuing investigation. Please question your child to see if he or she has been a witness to any crime or if he or she has been a victim . . . Also, photos may have been taken of children without their clothing.

The letter asked parents to ascertain whether their own children had ever seen Ray Buckey leave the classroom holding a child by the hand. It asked parents not to discuss the case with anyone outside their family circle. But the parents spoke to their children and to each other, starting a domino effect. A rumor started to circulate that in Manhattan Beach alone, which at the time had only around thirty thousand residents, 1,200 children were victims of satanic ritual abuse. A gynecologist concluded that 80 percent of the 150 children examined had experienced violent abuse. Dr. Pazder—by now a nationally renowned expert—consulted on the trial, in which seven preschool employees were charged with over three hundred counts of molestation. The testimony in each case was more bizarre than the last. One child said that after their mother had dropped them off at school, their teachers loaded them onto a plane and flew them to the desert. One of them claimed that Chuck Norris presided over the rituals. According to the prosecution, the preschool's motive was to make money by selling pedopornographic photos and films. But there was no proof or confirmation of this thesis. The McMartin trial was the longest in the history of the United States and concluded after seven years with the acquittal of all the defendants.

Meanwhile, a collective hysteria had developed, fueled in part by the media. TV personalities like Oprah started to host people on their programs who said they'd been part of sects that forced them to eat human flesh. On October 25, 1988, at eight p.m., NBC aired a controversial special called "Exposing Satan's Underground," where Geraldo Rivera examined the world of heavy metal and Haitian Voodoo to demonstrate the theory that Satan and his followers had fully infiltrated American society.

Rivera was harshly criticized by papers like the *Washington Post*, which in an op-ed titled "The Devil to Pay," accused him of making his fortune "with a series of cheesy, sleazy syndicated specials exploring the twilight zones of American society." But the program brought in stellar ratings.

Rivera wasn't the only soldier waging an antisect crusade defending Christian conservative values in an age of full-on Republicanism. Gordon Coulter, a police officer and preacher who called himself an expert on the subject, provided police precincts with a video tutorial on how to recognize occult symbols in their cities. It included images of the famous pentagram—the satanic inverted five-point star—as well as ropes, bottles of anesthetic, and various types of candles. Coulter also created a film set made up of two fake Greek columns and a bed. A bikini-clad model, whose body was covered in signs drawn with a marker, was laying down on the bed. This was supposed to allow officers to identify cases of suspected ritualistic murders.

The satanic terror didn't spare children's publishing, either. The illustrated book *Don't Make Me Go Back, Mommy* was released in 1990 as "a child's book about satanic ritual abuse." The psychosis also touched large multinational corporations like Procter & Gamble. Some people put forth the idea that their logo—a bearded man looking at the stars—contained references to the Devil.

In the 1980s and 1990s, American preschools were rife with these beliefs. They started a wildfire that took society back centuries. After the 1950s, daycare centers started popping up everywhere as an increasing number of women found work and needed institutions that could take care of their children while they worked. These institutions were often family run. After the McMartin trial, hundreds of copycat cases started to fill local and national papers. Gerald Amirault ran the Fells Acres Daycare Center in Malden, Massachusetts, with his mother and sister. They were accused of raping children with knives and forcing them to watch them sacrifice birds. The Kellers, who owned a preschool in Oak Hill in Austin, Texas, experienced an even more incredible accusation. Three little witnesses, whose parents were in touch with the families of the McMartin preschool children, said the Kellers tore animals and babies to pieces in front of them. Just as in the McMartin case, they said that they'd witnessed exhumations—similar to what Dario, Marta, and Margherita had said—and that they'd been taken from school and put on a plane to Mexico, where soldiers raped them on a military base. Then they returned to school just in time for Mommy and Daddy to pick them up in the afternoon. The Kellers were convicted in 1992 after a six-day trial. They received forty-eight years in prison. The truth came out much later, in 2009. The young psychologist who'd examined "patient zero" and confirmed the suspicions of his mother and the police, told the *Austin Chronicle* that he'd been wrong. At the time, he didn't have enough experience to recognize what was in fact a perfectly normal clinical profile.

All these American stories start the same way and follow a similar path: a mother is worried about her child's sudden change in mood, she decides that he was abused, and she turns to a psychologist for help. This is incredibly similar to what happened in the Bassa in 1997, when Mrs. Tonini noticed that Dario was tired, having trouble paying attention, and tripped a bit more than usual. Was something the matter? What was it?

"Come on, you have to tell me."

"Igor's games under the covers."

Games under the covers. Mrs. Tonini immediately interpreted this as synonymous with abuse and assumed the child just didn't know how to say it. She went to Dr. Donati, and together they harangued the child with questions. After that, like all the "patient zeros" of the world, Dario named names: Igor, Romano, Adriana. In no time, the phenomenon was creeping to other families like a dense, black fog and sparking a chain reaction. Case after case was falling onto the desks of detectives and prosecutors, whose research and investigations led them down a rabbit hole of fantastical memories of masks, butchered birds, excrement pies, videos of erotic games, and flying people. They were seeing the familiar traits of a worrisome social phenomenon that was very similar to Europe's *caccia all'untore* of the sixteenth and seventeenth centuries, when anyone suspected of spreading the plague would be hunted down. In 1992, FBI agent Kenneth Lanning published a report that expressed strong doubts about the existence of ritual violence. Reports were piling up in police stations from the Pacific Coast to the Atlantic. "One mother told me that for the first time since the victimization of her young son she felt a little better," Lanning wrote. Before then, her options had been to face the fact that her son lived in a community controlled by Satanists or accept the idea that he was a pathological liar.

Lanning's analysis was shocking. But however paradoxical it may seem, this psychological mechanism has been affecting us since the dawn of time. It's like the Jewish ritual of the scapegoat, in which the animal was laden with all the evils of a people and sent into the desert. This allowed the community to consider itself purified. By the same token, parents unable to make sense of common phases of discomfort and distress in children try to pin their problems and anxieties on someone else.

Lanning concluded his report by asking, "Are we making up for centuries of denial by now blindly accepting any allegation of child abuse no matter how absurd or unlikely?" The same question was asked in 1994. The National Center on Child Abuse and Neglect hired a team of experts to analyze more than twelve thousand cases of ritual abuse. They didn't find a single shred of proof to confirm this so-called satanic ritual abuse.

"Finding the bad guy restores peace of mind," Giuliana Mazzoni told me. She is a world-renowned professor of psychology who specializes in mass psychosis. "It restores the ability to live with oneself and not have to say, 'It's my fault.'"

The groundswell of cases was causing growing skepticism, especially among scientists. Nevertheless, America's paranoia began to cross national boundaries at the start of the 1990s, when it arrived in the United Kingdom. Mazzoni told me that many of the British communities that succumbed to it had recently hosted seminars where experts—or alleged experts—"basically told teachers and parents about the existence of collective sexual abuse based on Satanism, and they invited parents, teachers, and social workers to question the children, without actually teaching them *how* to question the children. And it's extremely curious how a few months after these seminars, the reports started to rain down."

Preschools weren't the only ones to end up in the crosshairs of investigators and prosecutors. Sometimes, the inquiring eye of the law rested on entire families. Some cases were almost identical to the ones in Massa and Mirandola. In the early 1990s, a seven-year-old near Rochdale, near Manchester, started to tell stories about ghosts. Teachers and social workers found this alarming and soon became convinced that they'd discovered a sect of rapists and Devil worshippers. Four children were taken away from their mother, then they started to give names. About twenty children in total were taken away from their families. In South Ronaldsay, the southernmost isle of the Orkneys, in Scotland, police and social workers took nine children away from their families in the dead of night. Upon being questioned, the children pointed the finger at a local priest, Reverend Morris McKenzie. As with Don Giorgio, Reverend McKenzie had provided financial help to the first families to be accused. It was said that McKenzie wore a hooded robe (as Don Giorgio was claimed to have done) and that he took the children to an open mine, where he and the children's parents lit large bonfires and danced bizarre dances while wearing masks—similar to the ones Margherita said she'd seen in the cemetery in Finale Emilia. The children said the priest picked up the children, one by one, with a long, curved shepherd's crook. But in this case, investigators were immediately suspicious of these accounts. There are very few trees on the Orkneys, and large nighttime bonfires would have been seen from miles away. A few months later, the children were returned to their homes. Celebratory crowds met them at the airport in Kirkwall.

Fear of the Devil took flight for a new destination, and a few years later, it landed in Bologna. On February 22, 1996, *La Repubblica* published an article that read like a review of the latest horror film to hit the theaters:

> **A three-year-old boy, locked in a dark coffin, imprisoned in a grave during a satanic ritual, with a skull in his hands. "Let's play a game," they told him. "Like at the movies." And like a good boy he obeyed, at least the first time. His "aunt's" friends certainly didn't want to hurt him. So he slipped in between the marble walls of the burial recess without a peep. And he let them lock him into the small coffin.**

The child's "aunt" was Elisabetta, a family friend who looked after him during the day. She was sixteen years old and a member of the Children of Satan, an organization founded by Marco Dimitri and known in the Emilian underground for holding summoning rituals in the countryside, in abandoned houses and in a little temple with images of the Devil. They were not worshippers of evil, but followers of Aleister Crowley's philosophy, which seventy years before had brought the word of hedonistic Satanism to northern Sicily. After Elisabetta reported being drugged and raped by members of the sect, prosecutors in Bologna turned their attention to that little three-year-old boy. His vocabulary was still very basic, but he'd managed to reveal incredible acts of violence. Dimitri and his followers were also accused of human sacrifice. But at the trial, prosecutor Lucia Musti's entire case collapsed. It had practically no evidence to support it, and Elisabetta often contradicted herself. She was later found not to be credible.

In June 1997, after months of media attention, Marco Dimitri and the Children of Satan were acquitted. At that very moment, some forty miles away, in a room at the Cenacolo Francescano in Reggio Emilia, a bespectacled blond boy who was a bit *straminato* was talking to a young psychologist from Mirandola and prosecutors from Modena. He was giving up the names of a new cast of monsters, the Pedophiles of the Bassa.

PART IV

THE TWENTY-YEAR-LONG NIGHT

14.

Finding "patient zero." Finding Dario. It was the first goal Alessia and I set for ourselves when we started looking into this story. Everything had begun with him. Yet our documents contained very few statements made directly by him. Most of what we had were transcripts from a meeting with the judge about preliminary investigations. The rest of his declarations had been reported through the mouths of Dr. Donati and Mrs. Tonini. Dario was like a ghost. A hologram with no voice, unable to give his version of events. We couldn't for the life of us find an exhaustive, authentic account given by him in the first person, without any filters. What did he remember of those difficult months? What did he think of this absurd, twisted story? I really wanted to know. But tracking him down also raised a significant ethical dilemma. What right did I have to knock on his door and make him relive his trauma? I meant nothing to him and had nothing to do with his story. I had no idea how he'd fared in the following years, or what kind of therapy he'd undergone, or whether he'd learned to manage his trauma and nightmares as he got older. Was it right to burst into his life without considering his feelings?

After Dario's revelations of abuse, cemeteries, and ritual killings came to light between February 1997 and October 1998, his world transformed into a house of mirrors. His perceptions were forever altered. The concepts of real and imaginary were now fused into one big caldron of nightmares, anxieties, and fears of persecution, making him even more unstable. And even more insecure. And maybe even more alone.

When Mrs. Tonini learned that Giorgios One and Two had found Dario at his school in Pegognaga, with the alleged complicity of Rita Spinardi, she went into a frenzy. The news traveled fast among the parents, creating a climate of suspicion that spread to the students. They, too, had been kidnapped—Dario had seen them at the cemetery. Mrs. Tonini couldn't take it anymore. If she let Dario stay in that school, she would be risking the lives of her entire family.

Social services helped her enroll him in another school, in Gonzaga, not too far away. During Dario's first day of school, Principal Ines Monti was approached by the *carabinieri*. "Are you sure you can adhere to security regulations?" they asked. "The child is not allowed to see anyone." Ms. Monti didn't understand the reason for all these precautions, or why the social workers from Mirandola looking after her new student were so obsessed with his protection. They even told her staff that doors and gates always needed to remain closed. A few days later, she stopped by Dario's classroom.

"How is he?" she asked his teacher, Ms. Marinella. "Is he fitting in well with the class?" Ms. Marinella said that Dario was a bit unusual. He had moments of "zoning out, of melancholy," and sometimes she had to call him back to reality. Ms. Monti suddenly felt someone pull on her jacket. It was Dario, looking at her intently. "Who are you?" he said. Ms. Monti was surprised.

"I'm the principal." But this wasn't enough for Dario. He wanted to know exactly what she did and where her office was.

"Why don't I ever see you? What's your name?"

"Monti."

"What's your first name? What is it?"

"Ines."

Soon after, Dario accused her, too. He'd seen her in the cemeteries in Massa Finalese. She'd even threatened him once. And a man with a goatee and longish hair with gray streaks had particularly agitated Dario. He was a count, and he conducted satanic rituals in the Gonzaga cemetery. Dario seemed to know the area well. He said he'd seen a "door in the ground with some stairs" and the remains of a child who'd been killed. The count was the father of one of his classmates. The forensic unit had found a small trace of blood on the hood of his car and immediately had it analyzed: it was of animal origin. The man was indicted in Modena. He was asked to state exactly how far his house was from the cemetery and to explain to prosecutors and judges why he had blood on his car.

"I assume it was a cat, since it was animal blood."

"Had you noticed this stain before police arrived?"

"Yes."

"You'd already noticed it?"

"Yes."

"Why didn't you clean it off?"

"Because I would have had to go to a car wash."

Another day, also in Gonzaga, Dario told Mrs. Tonini that a man "with a gun" had approached him as he left school. This was too much. Mrs. Tonini was exhausted. They had to get away. All of them. Her, Dario, and the other two foster children. She talked to her husband about it. They couldn't stay in that area anymore. It had become dangerous.

Mrs. Tonini turned to a close friend who had family in Crema, in the province of Cremona. An apartment had become available in their building. The Toninis moved in immediately and enrolled Dario in a public school. He seemed to like it. Maybe—finally—their family had gotten enough distance from those places to find some peace of mind. But then, once again, Dario started showing signs of distress.

Giovanna, his new math teacher, told him he was worthless. She punished him constantly and humiliated him. Mrs. Tonini met with her, but she denied ever saying or doing anything to Dario. That's when Dario added a worrying detail: one day, Giovanna had called him out of class so he could talk to someone on the phone. Rita—who by then was already on trial—spoke to him from the other end. She told him not to say anything and to talk to no one. And she wasn't the only ghost from the past to make an appearance. Dario had also seen Ines Monti, the principal from Gonzaga, standing in front of his school in Crema. She'd apparently followed him there. The boundless network of mean teachers and friends of Satanists had found him again, more than seventy-five miles from home. Moving had been useless.

Mrs. Tonini was desperate. Furious. "They followed him to this new school, they called him . . . and once again, he wasn't protected," Mrs. Tonini said during the trial to explain why she'd decided to suddenly remove him from that school, too. She then enrolled him in his fourth school in less than a year. This time, he was at a private elementary school, still in Crema, where Mrs. Tonini assumed he would be more closely monitored than in the public schools. Not so. A few days after classes began, the bishop of Crema, Monsignor Angelo Paravisi, went to visit the children to wish them a happy Easter. As soon as he walked into the classroom, Dario recognized him. He'd seen him at the Massa Finalese cemetery during the rituals. And soon after the brief meeting in the classroom, the bishop's assistant approached Dario to threaten him. Monsignor Paravisi ended up among the defendants of Pedophiles-2. Prosecutors Claudiani and Carlo Marzella questioned him before dropping the charges against him. And it didn't end there. One afternoon, Giorgio One snuck into the private school in Crema, just as he'd done in Pegognaga months before. He'd befriended a teacher who'd helped him enter.

Mrs. Tonini gave up. She didn't know where to hide her foster child anymore. Those orcs seemed able to hunt him down to the ends of the earth. So, in the spring of 1999, two years after the Galliera family was arrested, Mrs. Tonini temporarily sent Dario back to the only place she thought he might be protected. The only place that was really monitored, with an entrance that was always locked, a high gate that was covered by a net, and brave, attentive sisters who watched over everything and everyone. The place where this whole odyssey had started, when on December 26, 1993, a three-year-old boy left Oddina Paltrinieri's house in tears. Mrs. Tonini sent Dario back to the Cenacolo Francescano.

That was the last record we had of his whereabouts.

Seventeen years later, I found myself typing his name into search engines and social networks everywhere, hoping to find traces of him. I spoke to Alessia about it at length. We decided that the best thing to do would be to give him and the other children the chance to see this story from a different perspective, now that they were adults with the ability to read case files with a critical eye. It would be painful, this was for sure. But maybe it would help shed some light on what really happened. We planned on moving cautiously. We promised each other that we would retreat at the first sign of discomfort.

But Dario couldn't be found. I didn't even know what he looked like. I'd found two people with his name who lived in Emilia Romagna, but they couldn't be him due to their age. If I wanted to find out where he lived, I would have to retrace the steps of his life from the beginning and meet with people who'd known him. Starting with his birth family.

The house on Via Abbà e Motto in Massa Finalese was the last known home of the Galliera family. It's a decrepit yellow building on a dirt road. You can get there by turning off the main avenue onto a country road with no trees and heading toward the town of Macchioni. The house stands at a bend in the road, empty and abandoned, shrouded in fog, surrounded by weeds. As I walked in, I stepped on shards of tile and broken glass. I tried to imagine how that unfortunate family had lived, hand to mouth, every day. When they didn't have money for cigarettes, they smoked butts collected from the side of the road.

The rooms were freezing, and the house had no heating. I wondered which one Dario had slept in when he came to see Romano and Adriana on weekends. I wondered what he'd seen or heard or suffered within those walls. Who knows who the Gallieras really were? I could only guess at their level of financial and cultural poverty given what I'd read in the reports and what I'd heard from the Massesi in the piazza. Rumors of incest between Igor and Barbara. Rumors that Romano, to settle his debts, offered up Adriana as payment. Rumors that Adriana and Barbara, mother and daughter, prostituted themselves by the park. Rumors of Romano loading Dario into his car along with a television and bringing him to the crook Fredone. Town gossip. As rumors jump from mouth to mouth, any truth that is left risks falling off somewhere along the way, and a word that sounds like *deprivation* suddenly becomes *depravation*.

Who could really say whether something had happened to Dario at home or anywhere else? The doctor who examined him right after the first reports of abuse said no. Then, social services stopped bringing children to him. He was replaced by Dr. Maggioni. It became clear that the concept of a medical opinion was relative in a court of law. As was the opinion of a psychologist. Or a conviction. Or an acquittal. Seen from a few dozen feet away, in the fog, the house on Via Abbà e Motto seemed like the perfect symbol for such an absurd story. Crumbling and worn by time, it was far from everything and everyone. A red STOP sign was leaning against the building, signifying nothing. Windows were walled up or installed asymmetrically. It was as if the whole house had been designed by a child.

The last of the family to live there was Romano Galliera. Adriana was last there in 2009, when she was taken home from a prison in San Quirico, in Monza. Her hair was gray, she was full of tumors, she weighed a little over sixty-five pounds, and she was so weak she couldn't stand. They'd released her early on humanitarian grounds. She complained that she'd been subjected to duress for more than ten years after her son's declarations. "They wanted me to confess to burning children in the *stufa*!" she told anyone who would listen.

Romano followed her five years later, felled by a tumor on his only working lung. He is buried in the cemetery in Massa Finalese beneath a simple and spare wooden cross, drenched in humidity, among marble tombstones. It contains a laminated picture of a seventy-six-year-old man staring at the lens with intense blue eyes.

ROMANO GALLIERA

18-7-1937 17-1-2014

Nobody seemed to know where Igor and Barbara were. I'd heard that Igor had done about a year in prison. I found something that might have been Barbara's Facebook profile, even though it just contained pictures of flowers. And anyway, a message over the internet, especially when talking about such delicate matters, is never the best way to approach someone. Better to do it in person, or at least over the phone.

I reached out to the neighbors who'd helped the Gallieras right after their eviction in September 1993. Oddina Paltrinieri had died a year before, after a long illness, leaving behind her husband and two adult daughters, Giulia and Claudia. When I showed up, they were very welcoming, even though they initially looked at me with suspicion. They didn't understand why a journalist from Milan would be so interested in that story, to the point of coming all the way there so long after it had ended. But even though they didn't know or didn't remember many aspects of the case, they remembered their mother's obsession with it. Like Don Ettore Rovatti, she knew everything about the case of the Pedophiles of the Bassa. She'd kept newspaper clippings and never passed up the chance to talk about it with anyone who might be able to spread the word.

By all accounts, Oddina had had a strong sense of social justice. She was always on the front lines helping anyone who needed a hand. When that social worker arrived with a ruling on December 26, 1993, and took little Dario to the Cenacolo Francescano, she, Silvio, and their daughters had felt like they'd lost a member of their family.

That strange and dazed little boy had only been with them for three months, but he left a gaping hole when he went away. The family still felt the loss more than twenty years later—Silvio especially. He looked like a big bear and oozed the type of wicked irony that is common in rural Emilia. But whenever the conversation turned to Dario, he couldn't hide the sparkle in his eye. Photos of Dario were still hanging on the kitchen walls from the brief time he'd been with them. The family had also kept two home videos of Dario. They were in a corner among some old movies.

Silvio pulled out a dusty old VCR player from the basement. "*Prova mo' a vedere se funsiona ancora*," he said. *Let's see if it still works.* He shrugged, as if to say he wasn't handy with that type of technology.

The cassettes were damaged, but you could still see everything. There was Dario at daycare in Massa Finalese during a Christmas party in 1993, a few days before they took him away. He was sitting among dozens of children in white outfits with ladybug shells on their backs. They were impatiently waiting for the arrival of a slightly clumsy Santa Claus, who was pulling presents out of a bag. Little screeches of excitement drowned out the background music.

There was a video of them having lunch in their kitchen. Dario was sitting at the table wearing a red-and-blue tracksuit and playing with a toy race car. Silvio picked him up and asked him to sing something.

Dario looked so small in Silvio's giant hands. He stood on a bench and started to sing a song from Zecchino d'Oro. "Move your hands!" Oddina said to him. Dario flailed around before diving into Silvio's arms. In the following scene, everyone was around the Christmas tree, and Dario was strutting around the room in his new red jacket, tripping as he went.

"Am I handsome?"

"Not really!" Oddina joked while lying on the couch. She straightened his collar. Memories from long ago. Soon after, Silvio, Oddina, and their daughters watched from a distance as Dario morphed into a different person. They looked on in horror as their acquaintances were handcuffed or splashed all over the papers or had their children ripped away from them. The Paltrinieris never saw or heard from Dario again. But they'd stayed in touch with Barbara and Igor. The Galliera siblings had always been grateful to Oddina for all those times she'd shown up at their door with a pot of pasta or with some money to help them make it one more week. "If you want, I'll introduce you," said Giulia, the eldest daughter.

Igor lived fifteen minutes outside Massa Finalese. He didn't have a car. He didn't have a house. He didn't have anything. He lived in a squalid apartment in the projects. It was full of images of the Madonna. He lived off occasional work at a dump. A bachelor at forty, with a miserly stipend, he was accustomed to keeping his expectations low. The curse of being a Galliera. Maybe that's also why he didn't want children. We parked in front of the Finale Emilia castle to talk. The car windows were fogged up, and rain was tapping on the glass as Igor told his story to Alessia and me. He was direct and free of self-pity and spoke in a voice that was too wide and too deep for such a scrawny man. Igor's face was thin and pale, hollowed out by years of depression. His mouth was almost toothless from a losing fight with periodontal disease. He came off as someone who had started to wait for the end from a very early age.

I was curious to talk to him. Of all the people put on trial, he was the only one to have made a partial admission. He'd told investigators that he and his brother had touched each other, but only because Dario wanted to.

"Nothing ever happened between me and my brother," he answered decisively, in a slightly annoyed tone. "I swear."

Based on what he told us, Igor and Dario were often together when their parents weren't home. They were fifteen years apart, but they got along really well. They watched TV, they played video games. Dario liked one where you had to kill monsters. Or sometimes, he said, "We bought him things to color, and he'd spend some time up there, while I helped my dad split wood. Because we had to use the wood-burning stove . . ." Dario almost always slept with his parents. They all liked it that way. It was better than leaving him with his immature older brother, who one time almost set the sheets on fire after fumbling around with a bed warmer. He could have burnt himself badly. Sometimes Igor bathed Dario, when needed. And those were the only times he'd touched him. Nothing else. So what was Dario talking about when he said "games under the covers" with Barbara?

"I took the blame for something I never did. For touching my sister's leg."

"Why did you do it?"

"Because I was scared. I wanted to do less time. When they arrested me, I read something on the paper where they take your thumb prints and found out why. I read that word . . . but I had no idea what that word, the word *pedophilia* . . . I had no idea what it meant. They told me when I was in there. The lawyer said, 'I think you're guilty.' And I rightly continued to say, 'But I didn't rape anyone, I didn't touch anyone.' I said it over and over again. I was crying, I remember. At twenty-two years old, you're still a kid. I didn't know what prison was,

I didn't know what the years were, I didn't understand anything at that age. So I pulled out the first dumb thing that popped into my head."

This was his version of events. He'd only ever tickled Barbara. Nothing else. Everything Dario had said had come from his imagination. Or from someone else's.

Nothing strange had ever happened in their family. No one had ever abused anyone. No one had ever done anything suspicious with a close relative. Romano had some porno magazines hidden away in a corner. Maybe Dario had found them and flipped through them? Igor himself had done it fifteen years earlier. Could a little porno magazine really unleash a tsunami of that proportion? I didn't know if he was telling the truth. It was impossible to say. I wasn't going to judge him. I wasn't there for that. Then Alessia asked him if he missed Dario. Maybe for the fiftieth time over the course of our conversation, Igor shrugged and curved his mouth into an expression of feigned indifference. "Sometimes."

In 2009, when Adriana had only a few months left to live, Romano asked Igor and Barbara to give her a present. He wanted them to look for Dario, now an adult, so she could say goodbye one last time. They'd found him in a town outside Reggio Emilia, as he was walking home. He was still blond. He was taller than them. He wore jeans and a blue bomber jacket, and a quiff like all the nineteen-year-olds had at the time. He looked a lot like his mother. And like Igor. When he saw them, he seemed calm, despite all that had happened. Until his phone rang. It was Mrs. Tonini. Someone had told her that Dario had been approached by strangers on his way home. He immediately became agitated. He had to go home, or she'd get angry.

"We spent five, ten minutes together. We took a photo. I had it framed," Igor said with a sigh. "Then we left, and we haven't seen him since."

In the picture, Dario is standing between Igor and Barbara, with his arm around each sibling, a hint of a smile on his lips. But his gaze is turned to an indistinct point in the distance. Beyond the camera lens. A thousand-yard stare.

We met Barbara in the parking lot of a grocery store in a small town about an hour from Massa Finalese. Unlike Igor and Dario, she had inherited all of Romano's features, especially the small eyes and slightly bent nose. Life had been a bit kinder to her. She spent many years alone, waiting for her family to get out of prison. Then she met a man, and they got married and had a baby girl. Barbara also believes that nothing ever happened to Dario. No one ever touched him or did anything to him. The Toninis brainwashed him. They were the ones who planted all those stories in his head.

Her truth was that Dario wasn't happy with his new family. He hated it. He'd told her this one day while he was home, before he vanished completely. His foster brother, Matteo, who was a few years older than him, was beating him. The passing of the years and her extremely brief meeting with a grown-up Dario hadn't broken Barbara's hope of reconnecting with the person she called "my little boy."

"I miss him," she said, the old pain resurfacing in her sobs. "I don't know . . . To see him, to hug him, make him understand that I'm here if he needs me. I want to tell him that what he heard isn't true. We never hurt him . . . Now that Mom and Dad are gone, I wish the three of us could be together again."

But she had no idea where he was. Dario no longer lived in the town where they'd found him a few years before. He'd vanished completely. Again.

15.

One of Oddina's boxes contained a stack of letters the Gallieras had sent each other during their years of incarceration. I spent an entire night reading through them, in the living room of the little yellow house on Via Volta. There were dozens of them. The handwriting was sometimes hesitant and messy, sometimes rounded and crude. But between the lines was the emotional thread that tied four desperate people together. There were pages and pages of affectionate words, encouragement, reciprocal support, promises that "everything will be OK, and soon we'll all be together again." But there were also long rants of rage and frustration. After all, they were writing from behind bars. "I'm tired, because the months go by, and I don't see any changes, and I'm losing patience," Adriana wrote to Romano in a letter from Monza. "My love, I'm not mad at you but with those people that destroyed our family. It's hard to be in this place without having done anything. I love you." Romano was less prone to epistolary flourishes, but his writing clearly showed an honest, if clumsy, attempt to express his feelings for his children, especially in his darkest moments.

Oddina had also kept a lot of documents about the trials, including carefully stored newspaper clippings. Ever since Dario was taken, she'd been fighting her own personal battle against social services. She blamed them for not letting her take care of Dario and for leading him into madness. She wrote letters and emails to members of parliament on all sides of the political spectrum. She researched the people involved: the psychologists from Mirandola, some of whom she'd grown up with in

Massa; the ones from the Hansel and Gretel Research Center in Turin; and other experts she believed had contributed to building a case out of thin air. When the trials began, her little yellow house became a meeting point for lawyers, local journalists, and psychologists consulting for the defense. They all sat around the kitchen table, and between a glass of Lambrusco and a serving of pumpkin *turtlèin* with *ragú*, they talked about what could be done or exchanged the phone numbers of experts Oddina had found. She often stayed up late writing notes or searching for similar cases in other parts of Italy. She then reached out to the lawyers and families of the children involved.

One of these was Angela Lucanto, a seven-year-old girl from Milan. In November 1995, a teenage cousin of hers with psychiatric problems accused her whole family of abusing her, claiming that Angela had also been a victim. Just like that, without even investigating the matter in detail, a social worker and two *carabinieri* took her from school and brought her to a center for victims of child abuse. A psychologist asked Angela to draw a ghost. The psychologist thought the ghost looked like a phallus. Then a gynecologist—Dr. Maggioni again—speculated that Angela presented signs of sexual violence.

Her father ended up in prison but was acquitted after two and a half years. In the meantime, the juvenile court had ruled that the girl was "adoptable." Her parents and brother searched for her for years, until they finally found her one day on a beach in Liguria with her new family. She was already seventeen by then. She'd been waiting for them since the day she was taken away. She wanted to know why they'd abandoned her. For more than ten years, social services had threatened her and tortured her psychologically. They would have said anything just to emotionally distance her from her parents. Including that her parents didn't want her anymore. Or that they were dead.

Oddina read about her in the news, reached out to her, and found out that, once again, the case was being followed by CBM in Milan. The main characters were different, but the circle of experts was the same.

There was an explanation for all of this. In those years, Italy was becoming increasingly aware that rape needed to be addressed with specialized tools. In 1996, just before the Pedophiles of the Bassa scandal exploded, the Senate approved Article 66 of the penal code. "Provisions against sexual violence," transformed the crime from "a crime against public morals" to "a crime against the person." Law 285 came the following year, leading to the National Fund for Childhood and Adolescence, which allocated resources to "plan interventions at the national, regional, and local levels" aimed at helping vulnerable youth. Centers dedicated to treating trauma and abuse began to receive funding, and specialized disciplines were increasingly in demand among prosecutors, courts, social services, and other support structures. Experts started to sign up to a new association called the Italian Coordinated Services Against Child Mistreatment and Abuse, better known by its acronym, CISMAI.

CISMAI is a network of antiviolence associations and centers around the country. Member organizations offer training courses that teach psychology interns, school staff, and health officials how to recognize and treat child victims of violence. They use very specific observational techniques and methods of listening and interacting that are based on the idea that children tell the truth and rarely lie. At the time, they believed that despite the few cases of pedophilia and satanic ritual abuse passing through the Italian court system, there was still a vast, underground world that remained mostly hidden. No one seemed to know its actual size. CISMAI asked members to sign a consent form that required them to use an intervention protocol based on the premise that children's behavior always displayed specific "psychological indicators" of abuse. "The more a child was damaged by abuse, the more his ability to remember and talk about it might be compromised," reads point 5.1 of the association's guidelines. In interviews with minors, psychologists must use an empathetic approach to help them talk about what they don't have the strength or courage to say on their own.

Soon, Oddina and the family lawyers started to connect the dots. They realized that many of the psychologists involved in the Pedophiles of the Bassa case orbited around CISMAI. Not only that, but the CBM in Milan was a member organization, and that was where Dr. Donati had trained to work with vulnerable children. The same center supervised and endorsed Dr. Donati and her colleagues' work with the children of Massa and Mirandola. The center's president, Professor Paola Di Blasio from Università Cattolica, was also a consultant for the prosecution in Modena. Cristina Roccia and Sabrina Farci, expert witnesses for preliminary investigations, belonged to the Hansel and Gretel Research Center in Turin, so they were also CISMAI members. They were the psychologists who interviewed the children after Dr. Donati. After that, the children's words had become fully fleshed-out evidence against the defendants.

What all these experts seemed to overlook was that the children's stories could have been contaminated in some way. Someone could have planted a seed in their memories. It then blossomed and grew over time until it devoured their real experiences, substituting them with something that was partially or completely artificial. This phenomenon has been studied for a long time in the rest of the world, but it remains underestimated, especially among psychologists who aren't familiar with the research on the mnemonic functions of the brain.

This is so-called false memory. In 1996, the American magazine *Psychology Today* published a long interview with Elizabeth Loftus, a university professor who'd declared, "Eyewitnesses who point their finger at innocent defendants are not liars, for they genuinely believe in the truth of their testimony . . . That's the frightening part—the truly horrifying idea that what we think we know, what we believe with all our hearts, is not necessarily the truth."

In the mid-1970s, Professor Loftus started conducting experimental studies on memory. She wanted to demonstrate that this psychic function was actually composed of extremely porous and delicate material. She showed volunteers videos of traffic accidents, then used a series of questions to test their ability to remember a scene they'd just witnessed. She realized that the answers to her questions could vary based on the wording of the questions she asked. To the question "How fast were the two cars going when they hit each other?" the volunteers generally gave a lower speed than if the question contained the phrase "when they smashed each other." A simple verb was able to alter a volunteer's perception of a memory, leading to a different answer. An answer that could determine a different outcome in a court of law.

Professor Loftus's research focused on the credibility of court testimony and of repressed memories. Freud first covered the subject in the early 1900s. After *Michelle Remembers* came out in the 1980s, psychologists and the media took a renewed interest in it.

In those days, psychologists widely believed that when a person—especially a child—experiences trauma, such as sexual abuse, their subconscious instinctively expels the memories, freezing them and storing them inside the brain as though in a safe. The victim then forgets them, but only superficially, because in the meantime the trauma still has a deep effect on the person's cognitive system. When that person later manifests symptoms of malaise and doesn't know why, they might chance upon a psychologist who believes in repressed traumatic memories. That psychologist might claim they can decrypt the combination to the safe and extract its contents while preserving the absolute authenticity of the memory.

This is exactly what happened in those preschools, when alleged recovered memory experts convinced thousands of children that they were hiding ugly memories somewhere in their heads, and that these needed to be pulled out at any cost and by any means. Psychologists used regressive hypnosis, anatomical dolls, drawings, and targeted questions to help children reconstruct a specific event or to confirm the stories of other children who had already been interviewed. It wasn't unusual for the therapists to be the first to mention satanic ritual abuse to the children.

But Professor Loftus and other researchers like her were starting to work against the prevailing winds. They were showing how memory can be easily influenced by imagination, feelings, and especially by interrogation methods. "New 'information' invades us, like a Trojan horse, precisely because we do not detect its influence," wrote Professor Loftus in the results of her famous "Lost in the Mall" experiment. Professor Loftus and her colleagues James Coan and Jacqueline Pickrell, now psychology professors at the University of Virginia and the University of Washington, respectively, presented test subjects with four events they'd experienced in childhood, one of which—the time they got lost in the mall, before their parents found them again—never actually happened. Some of the interviewees initially said they didn't remember the incident, but upon being questioned again, they corrected themselves. They then reconstructed an entire scene from nothing, enriching it with detail: they described the stores they saw while looking for their mom, the old lady who helped them, their fear, and the subsequent crying fit. After the participants repeated their story a few times, the false memory the psychologists had planted solidified in their minds, mixing with memories of real events.

The theory was fascinating. I started to talk about it with colleagues and acquaintances. Eventually, I found someone who was aware of harboring false memories somewhere in their mind. I had one, too. One evening when I was a boy, a friend and I went to the theater to see our favorite comedians perform. The show ended late, and as we left, my friend and I said goodbye and headed to our respective buses. The following day, my friend told me excitedly that as he was waiting for his bus, some of the comedians had walked by. Upon seeing that he was alone, they asked him if he needed a ride to the nearest metro stop. His story must have made an impression on me, because several years later, I wasn't sure whether I'd experienced the event myself or whether someone had told me about it. I remembered the bus stop and I remembered one of the comedians getting in his car and asking me, "Do you need a lift to the metro?" But that never happened. Not to me.

In the case of the Devils of the Bassa Modenese, false memories infected children who hadn't even been taken away. While I was looking for Dario's childhood friends, scouring the various cities he'd passed through while being chased by fears of persecution, I found a list of students from his elementary school class in Pegognaga. One of them was named Marco G. I called him one evening, explaining that I wanted to talk to him about an old story regarding one of his classmates. They'd been in first and second grade together between 1997 and 1999. Marco hesitated.

"You mean Dario?"

"Yes."

Pause. Breath. Then, in a faint voice, he said, "Oh no . . ."

I was shocked. Of course he remembered him. Before Dario changed schools, he and Marco had been desk mates. Marco had even gone to play at Dario's house a few times. But in just a few months, Dario had upended Marco's entire childhood. He was gasping as he talked to me. That name had caused him to plunge back into a nightmare from long ago. He thought he'd been able to lock it away forever. Yet now, almost twenty years later, a stranger had come to rummage through his memories again. Of course he remembered that wretched year and that little blond boy with glasses, who told strange stories. Dark stories. Horror stories. One day, Dario told Marco and their classmates that Rita, their teacher, had taken him to the cemetery. Marco couldn't remember exactly what he'd said, but he never forgot those stories. They'd affected him so strongly that they insinuated the same "memory" into his mind.

"I'm . . . sure that what I'm about to tell you never happened," he told me during our short phone call. "But I have a clear memory of

Mrs. Spinardi taking us to the cemetery at night, and opening the gate to let us in."

From what he was telling me and how he was saying it, I sensed that he'd probably never overcome the trauma from that period. I asked to talk to him again at a later date, but he never responded.

Memory had played an ugly trick on him, too.

Professor Loftus had been impressed by a survey where 22 percent of therapists claimed they encouraged their patients to "let the imagination run wild" in order to recover memories of past trauma. If it was possible to trick adults, it was even easier to trick children. Professor Loftus's research opened a new front in the world of eyewitness psychology at a time when the Satanic Panic phenomenon was leading tens of thousands of children each year to become involved in sexual abuse investigations. Meanwhile, Dr. Stephen Ceci at Cornell University in New York focused his studies on children. He created a very unusual experiment. Once a week, he and his team met with children younger than six years old. During their meetings, he would ask them if they remembered an incident in which they ended up in the hospital after accidentally sticking their finger in a mousetrap. The team asked the question multiple times during the meetings, leading more than 50 percent of the children—all of whom had initially denied the incident—to change their minds. They made up a story from scratch, and it became increasingly detailed as time went on. Dr. Ceci believed that the simple repetition of the same question could destabilize a child, insinuating doubt in their mind and leading to a small mnemonic short circuit that activates the imagination, which attempts to compensate for the missing memory. "We find nothing in a child's memory is impervious to being tainted by an adult's repeated suggestions," Dr. Ceci told the *New York Times* in an interview. "We find from reading transcripts of investigations that in many sex-abuse cases the adults not only pursued a hypothesis about what happened, but were sometimes even coercive in getting children to agree." The same happened with the McMartin case, where children were asked "closed" questions that already assumed the existence of facts the children hadn't even mentioned yet.

Interviewer: Can you remember the naked pictures?

Child: shakes their head "no."

Interviewer: Can't remember that part?

Child: shakes their head "no."

Interviewer: Why don't you think about that for a while, OK? Your memory might come back to you.

After being pressured over and over again with sentences like "the other kids remember," the child adapted his memories to match those of the others.

Interviewer: Who do you think was playing the horsey game?

Child: Ray and Miss Peggy.

Interviewer: Ray and Miss Peggy? Did Miss Peggy take her clothes off?

Child: Yeah.

Interviewer: I bet she looked funny, didn't she? Did she have big boobs?

Child: Yeah.

Interviewer: And did they swing around?

Child: Yeah.

Professor Loftus and Dr. Ceci—along with many other researchers who'd become increasingly interested in the "misinformation effect"—declared a bona fide war within the field of psychology, which split into two opposing sides. One side urged caution, preferring the use of interview techniques that prevented the risk of creating false memories—questions that were open rather than suggestive. The other argued that this approach tended to favor the abusers at the expense of the victims. The conflict was waged with statistics, studies, publications, experiments, and conferences. Each school of thought wanted to be seen as the most credible—they wanted their science to prevail inside the courtroom.

The same thing soon happened in Italy. In 1996, as awareness of the threat of child sexual abuse was reaching its apex and the word *pedophile* was increasingly appearing in national headlines, a group of legal experts led by psychologist, professor, and lawyer Guglielmo Gulotta drafted the *Carta di Noto*, a document containing guidelines for examining minors in cases of suspected abuse. It later became a milestone of legal psychology. One of the document's key points advised experts to "avoid, in particular, recourse to suggestive or implicative questions that assumed the existence of the very fact that was being investigated."

The protocol very clearly defined the role of court consultants who examined suspected victims. "The expert must not be asked questions meant to ascertain the truth from a judicial point of view." The job of the psychologist is to verify whether the minor is able to bear witness and can provide a version of events that hasn't been contaminated. It is not the consultant's job to establish whether the child was a victim of abuse. That is up to the court—and only the court. This approach stands in sharp contrast with CISMAI tenets, which many legal psychology experts have criticized for promoting potentially dangerous listening methods that are based on antiscientific theories and that risk influencing children and contaminating their memory. The resulting trauma could even mimic that of an actual experience of abuse.

CISMAI responded to these accusations in kind. They weren't the real threat to children. The real threat were the psychologists who put the rights of adult abusers and potential pedophiles above the rights of children. From their point of view, the *Carta di Noto* didn't guarantee the safety of the victims.

CISMAI's new president—Gloria Soavi, a psychologist from Ferrara who was elected in 2014—made no secret of this viewpoint during a long interview over the phone. "Our approach focuses on the child as a presumed victim, on their psychological state and the nature of their trauma, with the understanding that there cannot be absolute neutrality in a relationship with a child."

The child "as a presumed victim."

One afternoon, I was at Silvio's house, poring over some old articles from Oddina's archives when Giulia and Claudia told me that just before she died, their mother had made them promise to never throw away any of her documents. "That way, if one day some journalist is interested, you can give everything to him," she explained. As I drank yet another coffee, trying to put Oddina's folders into chronological order, I glimpsed Giulia coming down the stairs with a big, brown box. She'd just found it in the attic. "Look, this was among my mother's things."

There was no paper this time. These were old videos. Dozens of them. Each one was labeled with a name. *Marta. Margherita. Cristina. Veronica. Federico.* I picked up a random one. *Pietro.* I pushed the tape into the mouth of the VCR. I rewound it. I pressed play at a random moment.

Wavy lines appeared on the screen. Then the image became increasingly clear. A boy in a white sweater and a vest was sitting at a table in front of a piece of paper and a Bic pen. A microphone was hanging from the ceiling above his head. Behind him was a yellow radiator attached to a dark-gray wall. The boy was saying something. "With the first boy, I had to throw a knife into his heart, then with another one, the second one, I had to tie him to a cement block . . . with a firebrand, I had to leave it on the fire for an hour . . . and then with the third, I whipped him, and then that's how he died, and I had to put a knife in his back . . ."

I was sitting on the couch holding my head in my hands. My eyes were wide open, and my heart was racing. Incredible. There they were, the children. Months and months of reading their stories. And now I had them all here. With their eyes, their postures, their mannerisms, their facial expressions, their hesitations. Their voices.

I pulled out all the tapes and stacked them on the wooden table in Silvio's dining room. I counted them: fifty-six, filmed over the course of about four years. The equivalent of at least eighty hours of interviews between the children and the expert witnesses for the prosecution and the court. The children's meetings with Dr. Donati had never been recorded. One of the defense lawyers had left these tapes with Oddina, who'd probably watched each and every one of them.

"You can take them home and watch them if you want," Giulia said. I hadn't owned a VCR in years. And converting all that to a digital format would cost an arm and a leg. But Zia Maria, Oddina's sister, stepped up. She'd take care of it. "Don't worry," she said. "I have time. Just tell me what format you want them in, and I'll send them to you." I didn't know whether to be happy or surprised to have found a nearly seventy-year-old computer geek in the middle of the Emilian countryside. One Monday morning a few weeks later, a courier rang my bell to deliver a package. I sat down, opened my computer, and took a deep breath. Here were eighty hours of interviews I could watch, transcribe, and interpret. The stack of DVDs on my kitchen table looked like a mountain.

16.

Three adults waited impatiently in a room. The man in the cream-colored suit at one side of the table, on the left of the screen, was Alberto Ziroldi, the judge for preliminary investigations in Modena. Opposite him was a woman in her forties wearing a floral dress, the psychologist Anna Cavallini. Sitting next to her was Dr. Valeria Donati, a twenty-eight-year-old woman in a blue blouse, with short black hair and glasses. With them was a little blond boy in a dark polo shirt: Dario. The window behind him was open, probably to bring some relief from the muggy summer heat.

The judge spoke first. "You said some things that made the grown-ups worry . . . The things you talked about are very, very serious . . . I'm going to ask you some questions because on the other side of the camera there are people who don't know all these things . . . We have to be as precise as possible. OK?"

But Dario wasn't cooperating. He was distracted, he was playing with his microphone, he changed the subject. Mostly, he didn't seem to understand the importance of the meeting. He wanted to talk about his cat, Luna, who'd just had kittens. And about the fact that a few days later, he'd be going on summer vacation with the Toninis. The Gargano beaches awaited him.

Dario had started to tell Dr. Donati about the pedophiles only a few weeks before.

"I'm wondering. How were you doing when you lived in Massa?" the judge asked him.

"Bad."

"Why bad?"

"Because they were doing those things to me . . ."

"What things?"

"That they would put their . . ."

"They would put their what?"

"Their penis in my mouth, their penis in my butt."

"Who did?"

"My real parents."

Igor would do it before. After, it was Romano. "After what?" They asked several times. The boy didn't seem to know.

Instead, he answered questions no one had asked him. "At lunchtime there nobody eats ever, ever, ever."

He was focused on his drawing. The adults insisted. "After what?"

Dario looked uncomfortable. "I'm tired . . ." He wanted to talk about the beach and the sea. He wanted pencils for coloring. He wasn't listening anymore. His descriptions of the abuse at the Galliera home were limited to remnants of sentences repeated ad infinitum. He added no details. As if there hadn't been a before or an after. Only sexual violence summed up in less than ten words.

The Honorable Judge Ziroldi, Dr. Cavallini, and Dr. Donati took turns trying to get Dario to focus on the subject of their meeting. Their efforts went nowhere. The same thing happened when they asked him about Rosa and her partner, Ales, whom investigators had identified as Alfredo Bergamini. Rosa was a mean person. She'd taught his mother how to do those things. *What things? How? Where? When? In what way? For how much money?* Dario started stories but didn't finish them. He asked if he could sit in Valeria's lap.

Ziroldi admonished him. "The beach is getting further away, buddy . . ."

This made Dario seek reassurance. "So, when I'm done with everything, I can go?"

"Yes, you can go, you can go to the beach then." Their urgency was palpable. As was their frustration whenever Dario became distracted. "The faster you tell us, the sooner you can go to the beach, got it?" continued Ziroldi.

Dr. Cavallini tried to prod him. "The sea is so blue there!" she said.

And then Ziroldi added, "But first, you have to help me out, buddy, or else . . ."

And again, Dr. Cavallini: "Come on, flex those little muscles . . . If you can tell us everything that really happened, you'll walk out that door and enjoy volleyball, the beach, and everything else so much more . . . You'll look at your muscles and think: *Wow, I was really strong!*"

Then Dario: "Do we have to stay here long?"

And the judge: "The sooner you answer, the less time you'll stay."

And again, Dr. Cavallini: "You're not listening. You're not listening! And this does you no good. It does you no good. Otherwise, we'll stay here a really long time, and you'll leave much later!" Dario was drawing a ship on a piece of paper. "That's a very pretty ship. Now, at this point we have to wait here for a while . . . You said that Ales took pictures . . . Who did he take pictures of?"

But Dario wasn't following. "I don't know what you mean . . ."

After an hour and a half, the judge and the two psychologists gave up. Dario could go to the beach.

Something wasn't right. I got the feeling that the adults weren't there to listen to him with an open mind or to understand if something had happened to him, but to make him talk, to make him repeat the same things he'd said to his foster mother and to Dr. Donati in the previous months. At the end of the interview, Dario formulated some extremely patchy accusations that if written down, wouldn't have filled a single page. Most importantly, it didn't contain a coherent narrative, or a beginning or an end.

I watched the video again, marking down all the times an adult had said the word *beach* to tempt Dario to cooperate or to use his vacation as a bribe: eleven times in one interview. If this was the method used in an official, filmed piece of evidence in the presence of a judge, what had happened when Dario had been alone with Dr. Donati? This video represented only the very first phases of the judicial process. Was this all it took to arrest all those people?

Since there seemed to be no trace of Dario anywhere online, I started to look into his foster family, who, in the meantime, had legally adopted him. An old article in an Emilia Romagna paper talked about the father, Mr. Tonini, being slightly injured after falling from a riding lawn mower. The article mentioned the name of the town where the accident occurred, a small village of fewer than twenty residents. Alessia, Giulia, and I arrived there one winter afternoon. Giulia had brought a photo album with some pictures of Dario from when he was little. When we got there, we asked some locals where the family lived, and we were told they'd moved to a town about fifteen minutes away. Dario's new home was in a white, two-story building a few steps away from a stream that separated it from a wooded area. A boy with olive skin was in the yard opposite the building. It was Matteo, Dario's adoptive brother, who'd also been raised by the Toninis.

"Is Dario home?" asked Giulia. "I came from Massa Finalese to say hi."

Matteo turned around and pointed to a woman leaning over a balcony. "You can talk to my mom." It was Mrs. Tonini. The woman immediately came downstairs and opened the door. She seemed agitated. Who were these people looking for her son after all these years? After all she'd endured to escape the demons that chased him?

"You shouldn't even know where he lives," she said. "This is very alarming. I ask that you immediately leave this house. Don't tell me anything else, don't show me any pictures, don't talk about me to anyone. I don't want to go down this road again. It's just too hard."

There didn't seem to be much room to maneuver.

"Leave now, don't tell me anything. I'm calling the police. I'm calling the police!"

Staying would have only made things worse. Better to leave. But we'd be back. We wanted to talk directly to Dario. He was twenty-six years old now and could decide on his own if he wanted to tell us his version of the facts or send us on our way.

A few weeks later, we got in our car and staked out Dario's building from about one hundred feet away, hoping he would walk out alone so we could approach him. We were sure that he lived there—Mrs. Tonini had let it slip during our brief encounter—but we didn't know his schedule. We showed up early one Saturday morning, thinking he'd almost certainly be home from work. Assuming he had a job.

It was raining, and the wait was grueling. For several interminable minutes, the cars speeding past us seemed to be the only things moving. Then, just before lunchtime, as I was scrolling through the news on my phone to pass the time, I glimpsed the shadow of a person crossing the path by the white house. He had a dog and was walking directly toward our car. I looked up, and for a fraction of a second, his face was just a few inches away from my window. I recognized him by his asymmetrical blue eyes, enlarged by a pair of very thick glasses. He had the same look as in Oddina's photos and videos. It was Dario.

With bated breath, Alessia and I waited for him to walk away. We wanted to keep his family members from seeing us speak to him. We didn't want him to feel uncomfortable. We got out and followed him from a distance. He was wearing a tracksuit, a wool beanie, and a jacket, the classic look of someone who is just running out on a brief errand. When we caught up with him and explained who we were and why we'd sought him out, he didn't seem afraid.

At twenty-six years old, he still hadn't found direction. He worked as a gardener whenever there was work, but he had no real plan in mind. As soon as we got the conversation going, he came out with a comment that left us speechless. "*Boh*, honestly, I'm not sure whether anything actually happened or not . . . Many shrinks also try to make you tell them what they want you to say, you know, for money, so I'm not sure anymore . . . I have some memories, but I don't know if they're real or not . . . I mean, as a kid you pull out whatever you want . . ."

"Patient zero," the voice that launched a thousand hurricanes, was questioning himself and doubting what he'd said. It was the last thing we were expecting to hear. Now that Dario could look at the past with the eyes of an adult, he seemed to have recast his experience. He didn't have good feelings for Dr. Donati, who'd treated him until he turned eighteen. He believed she used him to make money and advance her career, because after the children were removed from their families, she'd been promoted to an important position, and "she made a boatload of money," he said, though he didn't specify what he was referring to. He used the expression *brainwashing* twice during our conversation.

"The same people who tried to help me were also destroying my family," he added, alluding to a disagreement between Dr. Donati and Mrs. Tonini. His foster mother had started to work with Dr. Donati on a series of fostering commitments, but she hadn't been paid what she was owed. Dario didn't go into detail.

To him, it was all water under the bridge. He just wanted to forget the whole thing as soon as possible. Especially after changing schools and cities so many times. The fears of persecution had left him traumatized, which lasted well beyond his elementary school years. Dario spent his adolescence looking over his shoulder. "They also came looking for me when I was in middle school . . . I mean, all these people would come looking for me at school . . . Anyway, the teachers would keep them away. They always made sure they didn't see me. I had constant paranoia." He dragged his paranoia with him to Modena when he went to live there in his early twenties. He said, "I was sure they were going to come kill me" for some strange reason. He avoided taking regular routes. He didn't know anything about how the story had ended. He didn't know how many suspects had been involved, how many convictions, how many other children. His knowledge of the case was limited to his own involvement, and that was it. Thinking back to those years and the people he'd named, he could no longer distinguish between the facts and the nightmares, the real people and the visions, the scenes of the life he'd lived and the life he'd imagined. The abuse at the Galliera household—this he did remember, in "shreds." As for everything that happened after, he remembered very few things.

"Do you remember being in a cemetery?" Alessia asked.

Dario thought for a moment. "I remember it, but I mean, the walls, like stone walls . . . but . . . I mean, I don't even know if it was a cemetery or an old abandoned house, you know . . . I mean, I vaguely remember some things that . . . all these little red lights like . . . some colored windows . . ."

If the stories he'd repeated ad nauseam as a child only sparked memories of three, maybe four images, what did he remember of the events in the cemeteries?

"For example, do you think you really killed those children?" I asked him point blank.

Dario sighed.

"I do have the memory, because until five years ago, it weighed on me."

"Of having killed a boy in the cemetery?"

"Yeah."

"But you do know that they never found a body?"

"No . . ."

"You didn't know?"

"I mean, I more or less know that they nabbed some people, put them in jail . . . But that they never found anything? No, no one ever told me that."

Alessia and I had been the first to tell him that those crimes were only in his head. The psychologists who treated him during the case, especially Dr. Donati, never bothered to inform him of the outcome of the investigations. For the first time during our meeting, the blond boy in glasses and a wool beanie seemed relieved. Maybe now he could let go of the terrible sense of guilt that had destroyed his childhood and adolescence. Maybe he wasn't a murderer.

"What memory haunted you the most?" I asked him.

Dario went back to the beginning. There was an old pain he'd been holding on to for years. It wasn't persecution. It wasn't the satanic rituals. It wasn't the abuse. It was the clear, pure, real memory of a faraway morning on December 26, 1993, when he was only three years old and a social worker had shown up at Oddina's house, made him get dressed, and led him to an institute run by nuns, where he was forced to start a new life.

"The abandonment . . . When they took me to a place, and they didn't even stop to tell me what was happening . . . When they took me to the Cenacolo."

We agreed to see each other again in the following days. Dario wanted to know more, to go back to where it had all started, retrace his journey, understand what had altered the course of his life. We sent him some material on similar cases from the United States and the United Kingdom. We wanted to further reassure him that although he had some deeply embedded memories of massacres in cemeteries, those events had never really happened. This idea seemed to transform his life. He wrote me a message telling me those memories had led to him having a drinking problem.

Now, he was starting to feel a little better. He must have stayed up all night reading, because the following morning he wrote us a quick email:

> **of course a child would talk about make believe, after 8 hours of stress, and pressure u just want to go to bed. i'm sorry for all the good people that were arrested. until 3 years ago I still believed everything. or on the inside maybe u Don't know if it was real or not. but if u can't remember many things later u figure out that they used u however they wanted, or for their own ends. and I know I'm to blame, because I could have been taken away ok, but without getting people mixed up in it that never had anything to do with this story. Thousands of kids built it up again and again, just with different names. the leader of the rituals always with a strange name. in my case the devil. and the more u go on and the more you just hope that no one comes to give u the lesson u deserve. for me it's been a year and a bit since I've had serious doubts about it all. and I try to get by without giving it too much weight. but I'm mad at the people that used me!!**

Waves of memories started coming back to Dario after he'd stopped seeing Dr. Donati, confirming his growing doubts about the past. He hated the psychologists and social workers who'd treated him. Now, he felt like he was seeing things more clearly, though some of his messages seemed a bit manic. I calmly asked if we could meet for a coffee, but he suddenly disappeared. We didn't hear from him for a full day. Worried, we tried calling him a few times. His response was this:

> **Try to come to my house one more time and bust my family's balls and you'll see what you'll get. Stay**

> **away from me and from the people around me if you don't want trouble with the carabinieri. I don't want to have anything to do with my past, or with shitty people like you.**

A drastic change in attitude. Alessia and I guessed that someone had gotten to him. Dario wasn't answering our messages anymore, and it was useless to persist. Then, a few days later, Matteo wrote to us on Facebook. He had some important things to say and wanted us to call him. He seemed paranoid. He referred constantly to a fear of being killed or of being locked up in a psychiatric hospital by an unknown enemy without a face and without a name. It was just *Them*:

> **If nothing happens to me within 60 days I'll tell you everything I know, but if they do something to me show this message to your lawyers . . . They'll come tonight . . . for me it's over, if they don't kill me they'll make it look like a suicide . . . If I get through the night (which is unlikely) we'll find a way to meet . . . They're fucking me over big time, I got through the night but of course they'll get me during the day (they'll leave something for me at home and then they'll skin me alive with fake military/jail/suicide).**

It was a delirious shower of messages that combined to form a single, psychotic monologue. The only part that seemed to make any sense was this part about Dario: "At first he liked you guys, but then our mother told him you want to screw him over."

Mrs. Tonini and her obsessions, twenty years later. What was happening in that family? Was it a coincidence that both the children she'd raised felt like walking targets and were sure that someone wanted to kill them? After a few days, Matteo vanished, just like Dario had.

17.

My headlights lit up the dark streets of Mirandola as I drove. The city's historic buildings were still propped up by scaffolding after the earthquake, lending it a feeling of perennial instability. One of these buildings was a six-story, red brick condo on the corner of Via Pascoli and Via Statale 12. The Scottas had lived there, and it was where a desperate Francesca had thrown herself off a balcony after Marta was taken away. Like the Galliera house on Via Abbà e Motto, twenty minutes away, the building was a teetering carcass, an empty, fenced-in termite nest in the open country. They called it the *Excelsior*. I never understood why.

I drove past it and parked a mile away, in front of a house in a residential area. A man waited for me at the door. He had a wide forehead and a deep voice. He was forty-four years old. Carlo. He welcomed me with kindness, but I sensed some reticence. I wasn't alone. I had brought with me a story of pain and heartache from twenty years before. Since then, all his days had been filled with a deep bitterness.

"Come," he said. "Let's go. It's all up in the attic." We climbed a flight of stairs to an overstuffed attic.

"Please excuse the mess, but I just moved here, and I still have to organize everything."

He pulled out an old moving box. Inside was everything that remained of his mother, Francesca, and his sister, Marta.

"I'm sorry you have to see me this way," he continued. "But the other day, when you called . . . everything came out again, and I didn't feel well. Do what you have to do. I'll be downstairs if you need anything."

Carlo was twenty-four years old in 1997 and hadn't lived with his mother for some time. She'd raised him on her own, but that was before she found a new partner and had a second child. Marta was sixteen years younger than Carlo. But he loved her, even though he felt a bit jealous that she got all the attention. Unlike him, she was given everything. He'd nicknamed her *Capo*, "boss," because whatever Marta asked for, Marta got. But he often visited her and played with her. He adored her.

Around six twenty p.m. on July 7, he got a call from his mother. She was out of breath. That morning, they'd taken her little girl away. Carlo didn't know what to do. Every attempt to calm her, to persuade her to be patient, to tell her that everything would be OK fell on deaf ears. He went to the police for an explanation, but no explanation was given. He couldn't even find out where Marta was. "We can't give out any information. Investigations are ongoing." He raised his voice. That's enough. He was going to hire a lawyer. He was going to make a fuss. But then an officer he knew took him aside. "Stay out of this. Don't get involved or you'll end up mixed up in it, too. And you're not going to come out of it unscathed."

Carlo was scared. Best to stand aside and watch events unfold. Meanwhile, the papers were starting to cover the first leaks by the prosecution. Francesca had been accused of pimping out his sister. She allegedly took Marta to apartments packed with sexual deviants who paid her lots of money. Carlo was confused. Francesca had never done anything of the sort to him. She sometimes smacked him, sure, but she'd never gone beyond that. But doubt did creep in. The police, the papers, the social workers who called to question him were all asking: Who really was the woman who'd given birth to him? How did she treat Marta? Had he ever seen anything strange? The more he thought about it, the more he remembered his unresolved questions. For one, she'd never told him who his father was. Then there was the other great mystery he'd been holding on to all his life. Sometimes, when he was a boy, Francesca would come home later than the closing time of the bar she worked at. And the rumor was going around that she'd been a prostitute. Did he even know her?

Their relationship became tense. Francesca was on the verge of a nervous breakdown. She was always out, always protesting outside the police station. The police called him often. "Your mother's here again, please come talk to her. She won't leave. She wants to slit her wrists."

He went to visit her one day and found the door locked from the inside with a chain. Francesca wasn't answering the door or responding to him when he called to her. *Mamma, open up. Mamma, answer me. Mamma, where are you?* Nothing. Carlo called the police. An officer came and broke the chain by kicking in the door. His mother was face-down on her bed, unmoving but in agony. She'd taken a hefty dose of pills. They quickly loaded her into an ambulance and saved her life—barely—a few hours later in the hospital. Then, on a Sunday in late September, came another call from the police station while Carlo was at the beach with his girlfriend, enjoying one of the last warm weekends of summer.

"I'm at the beach," he said. "If it's not serious, I'll come by later."

It's not serious, they assured him. It could wait until evening. He arrived before dark. The first-floor lobby was full of chairs and gave onto a few offices. An officer walked up to him.

"Your mother's dead," he said. "She killed herself. I'm sorry." He patted Carlo on the back, turned around and left, leaving him there, speechless.

Francesca's apartment was seized by the police, but an officer allowed Carlo to come in and get his belongings. He saw some of Marta's things piled up in a corner, along with a box containing the only gold his mother had left. Bracelets, necklaces, a few rings. Next to it was a handwritten note. *Give this to Marta.* Every September 28, Carlo takes a train to Naples to spend a few hours in silence by Francesca's grave.

Carlo found no trace of Marta. No one could or wanted to help him find her. After a year at the Cenacolo Francescano in Reggio Emilia, she'd been placed with a foster family who lived in the area.

One day, Carlo typed her name into Facebook. The only result that came up was the profile of a girl with wavy brown hair and a silver nose ring standing by the beach and smiling. She was about twenty years old.

"Hi, I'm looking for someone who has your same name. I'm looking for my sister," Carlo wrote. The answer came swiftly: "I'm not the person you're looking for. I hope you find your sister." Then she blocked him. He knew it was her.

"Did you manage to find her?" Carlo asked me the first time I called him. I had. Alessia and I had gone looking for her at the nursery school where she worked, but her colleagues told us she'd just moved. They had her contact details. We found her house, a little place in rural Reggio Emilia. Her foster parents showed up at the gate, hounded us with questions, and asked us to leave. We withdrew and called her. Marta was nice, but firm. "I've already said all I have to say about this story years ago to whoever needed to hear it. I have nothing to add."

Carlo asked me if I'd managed to meet her in person. I told him I hadn't. If I thought there was even a remote possibility that Marta would reach out. I strongly doubted it. If it would be a good idea to show up at her house and ask her to reestablish a relationship that had been interrupted decades before. I had no idea.

The first thing I noticed when I opened the box was a pair of little red baby shoes stored in a rectangular see-through container. Then the pictures. A lot of pictures of mother and daughter taken throughout their eight years together. Francesca nursing Marta on the bed. Marta in her high chair. Marta taking her first steps. Marta playing with a dog. Marta at the beach, at home, on the balcony. They were often hugging. There was also an old red box containing a well-worn rosary and two or three images of the Virgin Mary. Some clothes. A little child's coin purse containing a five-thousand-lira note ($3). Two cream-colored ring binders, one with Marta's school drawings—*Mommy I love you*—and the other with old social services reports going back to before the pedophiles case, when Francesca and her partner had engaged in a bitter custody battle over Marta. The social workers had written that it was impossible to establish a dialogue with Francesca. The "Mrs." was possessive, uncooperative, and openly opposed to any decision the social workers made. Until July 1997, Francesca mostly fought Marta's supervised visits with her father. After that, a boy from Massa Finalese whom Francesca said she'd never even seen, gave her name in an interview. But this very naming—of Francesca and her friend, Federico Scotta—contained a clue that the prosecution and courts had inexplicably overlooked.

At the trial, Dr. Donati explained how Francesca and the Scottas had been identified. When Dario first told her that other children were involved, she tried to find out who they were. One day, "during a session, he asked me and his foster mother whether 'Chinese people have yellow skin.' He asked the question while drawing children playing soccer." Dario also asked whether, in addition to having yellow skin, Chinese people also had almond-shaped eyes. And if they were "green." Dr. Donati immediately became suspicious. "I connected all these facts, and I must report that little Elisa, whom I know, is a little girl with clear Asian somatic traits (her mother is Thai), and she has the distinctive quality of having eyes that are both almond shaped and green." She asked Dario if he'd wanted to know about Chinese people because he was thinking about a girl named Elisa.

The name hadn't come from him; it came from her. Dr. Donati was the one who had arbitrarily associated a banal question—on the shape and color of the eyes of an entire people—with a three-year-old girl with almond-shaped eyes who was in the care of those same social services. And then she'd submitted it to Dario, who confirmed it, which he often did. Even though it was obvious that he didn't know who she was, because during a photographic identification exercise, he'd confused her with another girl, Elisa's neighbor, whose mother was good friends with the Scottas. A coincidence? That girl was also being cared for by social workers. It was Marta. But even months after she was taken away, when she started to talk about her abuse and her abusers, Marta always denied knowing Dario. She repeatedly contradicted one of her own stories about going to the home of a priest who'd raped them both. But she didn't know Dario. She'd never seen him before. Investigators and psychologists found an explanation: Marta was resisting. She was struggling to get everything off her chest. Dario, on the other hand, was right. Always and forever. Prosecutor Claudiani said it himself in his report on the Pedophiles-2 trial. There was no reason to think otherwise.

I couldn't believe what I was reading. The monstrous mouth of that emotionally and psychologically unstable woman had launched police squadrons upon entire families, violently tearing them apart. Dario's words were used to divert and devastate the lives of others. Even his parents had been turned inside out as the police searched for clues.

Like when he first spoke about the rituals in the cemetery. It all started when he told Dr. Donati that he'd been to a funeral where a woman was carrying a coffin. He'd been impressed. Sometime later, as he was expressing his feelings to her, he said he was afraid of burning in hell. Dr. Donati created a bridge between the two words *funeral* and *hell.* "I asked him if this thing (hell) was connected to an old story he'd told me, where Dario had been to a funeral where he'd seen a woman carrying a coffin and had been very afraid. Dario answered, 'Yes, you're right.'"

That's how the hypothesis of the satanic rituals was born. Not from Dario's spontaneous account, but from an arbitrary association presented to him ready-made and tied together with a bow. A prepackaged storyline that just needed to be approved. *Yes, you're right.*

A few months later, Marta confirmed Dario's story to Dr. Donati. She repeated it to the consultants from the Hansel and Gretel Research Center in Turin in front of a camera. Again, the psychologists didn't seem interested in listening. They seemed to be looking for confirmation of an idea they already had clear in their own minds. In one of the videos from Oddina's archives, dated January 1999, Marta was wearing a red sweater and sitting in front of Dr. Sabrina Farci in an office in Mirandola. Marta hadn't been in her hometown since they'd taken her away a year and a half before. She seemed happy to be there.

"We even drove by the square," she said with a shy smile.

"You went by the square? What was it like, seeing it?" Dr. Farci asked.

"A bit emotional."

"Could you give a name to this emotion?"

"Joy!" Marta said. Dr. Farci clearly didn't like that answer.

"Maybe there's another emotion along with joy? Is there another emotion, or isn't there?"

Nope, just a bit of joy, Marta answered firmly, for the second time. Dr. Farci was starting to insert a new element into Marta's mind, something the girl had never mentioned before.

"Maybe there's also a grain of pain, coming back here. Could that be? Maybe it's just hard for you to say it. Maybe some things happened that are painful to remember."

Marta gave up and nodded. The rest of the video recorded her accusations against Francesca.

"So you were saying . . . your mom?"

"She took me to bad places, to the cemetery and to other people's homes."

"And what time did she take you to the cemetery?"

"Hmm . . . about evening."

"About evening."

"Sometimes in the afternoon, too."

"What happened in these places?"

"They hurt me . . ."

"Did they do it to everyone or just to some of you?"

"To all the children who came."

"Ah, did a lot of children come?"

"Oh, yes . . . And then at the end they gave money to my mommy."

"They gave money to your mom . . ."

"Uh-hm."

"You know, that is really sad. I understand, you know. It must be really hard for you. Maybe sometimes you were also really mad at your mom."

"Oh, yeah . . ."

"And you were able to express your anger only after she was gone."

"Uh-hm."

Here they were again. The insinuations. Suggestive questions. Dr. Farci was seeking confirmation, overlooking all the absurdities coming out of the girl's mouth—for example, that satanic rituals in cemeteries occurred "sometimes in the afternoon"—just so she could validate the thesis the psychologists had decided on beforehand.

Carlo had preferred not to watch the videos of his sister. Too many memories, too much pain. He wouldn't have had anyone to talk to about it, no one to vent to, no one who would understand his story or his drama. Maybe, he said distractedly as we said goodbye, he wasn't even ready to seek her out. He would stay there a bit longer, in limbo, hoping that maybe, one day, his doorbell would ring.

Until that moment, I'd been surprised by how much family members hesitated to go looking for their children. They were clearly suffering, to the point where all of them, in different ways and at different times, had sought some level of contact with their children, nephews, and nieces after they'd reached adulthood. But none of them followed up after that. Letters, postcards, messages on social media, a few attempts at phone calls—nothing more. At first, as a father of two small children, I couldn't understand why they'd be so hesitant. Instinctively, I thought that in their place, I would have searched for my children to the ends of the earth. I would have gone to them in person, implored them for five minutes of their time so that they could look me in the eye and hear my side of the story. I would have forced them, if nothing else, to hear my voice shouting my innocence, my pain, my truth. But then it became clear that their fear was hiding a defense mechanism by proxy, which protected their children from the consequences of such a choice. They were afraid of hurting them even more.

"Why don't you go to your children? What's holding you back?" I asked Lorena one day in her living room in Salernes. Every year since the removals, she'd sent letters upon letters and packages to her four children, without ever once going to knock on their doors.

"Well, I don't want to cause them more suffering. So I ask myself, do *they* need to see me? Do *they* need to meet me?"

An instinct of self-preservation was also holding them back. Many of the parents, including Lorena, felt victimized by a monstrous miscarriage of justice, and this framing had allowed them to survive their long years of solitude. Federico Scotta told me about it. He'd sent a message to Elisa on Facebook soon after she turned eighteen but didn't get a reply.

"The fear of being—how should I say—judged for the umpteenth time held me back quite a bit, because anyway, you know, it's hurtful to hear your child tell you, 'I don't want to see you anymore' or 'Who are you? You're not my dad. You're that guy who hurt me, you were supposed to protect me and you weren't there.'"

Many of them didn't want to risk destroying the tenuous, irrational hope that one day, their kids would come home. Life had condemned them to waiting. They had already been waiting for twenty years. And they would continue to wait. Some reciting rosaries every evening and every Sunday, some flipping through old photo albums day in and day out, some secretly following their children's lives on social media, looking at pictures of birthdays, graduations, engagements. Anything more would have been emotionally dangerous. I would have confirmation of this from one of the people I least expected: Elisa Scotta, a girl with straight brown hair and slightly almond-shaped green eyes who'd been trying to find her brother, Nick, for a lifetime.

When Alessia contacted her on Facebook, Elisa immediately agreed to a meeting. On July 7, 1997, when she was three years old, she was taken back to the same foster family that had temporarily cared for her after she was injured. They soon became her adoptive family. She hardly remembered anything from before. Her birth parents, Federico and Kaempet, were two faded shadows, faraway flashes of light that she couldn't make out. She'd had a happy childhood, surrounded by other adopted siblings who loved her as much as her new parents did.

But after twenty years, she started to look back and think about her past and where she came from. She'd read some things about the case of the Pedophiles of the Bassa, and she'd become curious when she found out that someone had referred to it as a "judicial error," a colossal case of suggestion on the part of the investigators. But that wasn't why she'd agreed to meet with me in a café outside Modena, surrounded by elderly men playing cards. She didn't miss her parents. She missed Nick, her little brother. He'd been just a few months old when she last saw him that morning in July, but she had a very clear memory of him. She had just fallen asleep in the waiting room at the Mirandola police station while Federico and Kaempet were upstairs. The head of social services, Marcello Burgoni, was handing them the ruling that would take their children away forever. When Elisa woke up, everyone was gone. Her parents. Nick. Someone had decided to split her and Nick up forever, placing each of them in a different family, giving each of them a new identity.

When she was twenty-two years old, Elisa had gotten in touch with Valeria Donati. She wanted help making sense of her past. She was told that it wouldn't be possible.

"I just want to find him," Elisa told me. She sounded like she'd spent her life thinking intently about someone unattainable. "Him and Stella." The younger sister who'd been taken away in the delivery room. All traces of her were lost. I promised Elisa that I'd try to find her. But I also wanted to understand how she felt about her mother and Federico. Elisa shrugged.

"I'm indifferent. I mean, it doesn't change anything for me. I can't go back. It stays there for me. I can't say I consider him a father, because he wasn't. I didn't have anything, and I don't want anything. I mean, he may be innocent or maybe not, but he let us be separated, and after everything that happened, we all ended up apart."

Her apparent unconcern was hiding a thinly veiled anger. Elisa had been holding on to it for years. She wanted to understand. She wanted to read the reports and make up her own mind about what had happened. She never said much to the psychologists as a girl. She only remembered telling Dr. Donati about a few kittens that had hurt themselves and needed to be cared for. Nothing else. She'd learned the rest later, from secondary sources. Meeting her birth parents wasn't an option at the moment. First, she wanted her siblings.

As for Nick, I only knew the name of the town he lived in and the pharmacy where Federico had thought he'd seen him years before. I searched online for the pharmacist's last name. I found an old junior soccer team in the area. The list of players contained their birth dates, including the one I was looking for. After a few clicks, the image of a young man with clear Asian features popped up on my screen.

Elisa was ecstatic. They had the same eyes. It was him. One evening, she built up the courage to write to him. But his answer hurt her. He thanked her for looking for him, he was pleased, but he had his own life now. He already had a family. He already had sisters. He didn't feel the need for another one. Elisa cried. She'd spent so many years looking for him, thinking about him. And now two simple lines on a page had ended everything. Elisa felt alone again.

"I don't miss my parents," she told us in tears. "I just miss my brother and sister . . . and that's it . . . because none of us children did anything to deserve this."

She wasn't the only one to have lost a sibling. The other children experienced the same fate. Social services and the juvenile court system had always been clear about their policy to burn bridges with all members of the birth family, including grandparents, uncles, aunts, and cousins. None of them were ever allowed the right to visit the children or to send letters, pictures, or presents.

18.

Dr. Donati always denied influencing the children in any way. Yet during her depositions, she sometimes let slip assertions that seemed to prove the exact opposite. I found one such assertion in a report from the hearings and circled it in bright red pen. It seemed significant. Maybe more than anything else, it unveiled the distorted mechanism that propelled this whole story forward. The prosecutor asked her how often she met with Margherita after she was taken away. "Same as the other children," Dr. Donati answered. "We see them once a week, except for when there's a special need for them to be seen. For example . . . to prepare them for a hearing."

Prepare her for a hearing. That is, before the children were taken to an expert witness for the court, who took their statements during preliminary investigations. What exactly did Dr. Donati have to prepare them for? To recite a script? That was my impression. Especially after watching the recording of one of Lorena's children, who at the end of his mad tale of multiple ritualistic killings asked Dr. Roccia, "Did I say the right thing?" As if looking for reassurance that he'd laid out the details properly.

Dr. Roccia had talked to Margherita, too. The Giaccos' daughter knew who she was even before meeting her. Dr. Donati had prepared her. "I heard that you talked to Valeria. You went to school with her," Margherita told Dr. Roccia during their first meeting. "Yes, we met in Milan. We were in the same training course on how to help abused children." A course held by CBM in Milan.

Then they got to the point. As with most of the children, Margherita seemed calm in front of the camera, listing traumatic experiences as if she were telling a fairy tale. But while her words expressed a fear of being hurt by demons, emotionally she gave no signs of this.

"What scares you about talking about these things?"

"That the Devil could come."

"So you're worried that the Devil could really get you. That means you're really good at hiding your feelings because if I thought the Devil could get me, I'd be really scared . . . But how do you defend yourself from the Devil? Is there a place you can go to feel safe, where the Devil can't reach you?"

"When I talk to the judge. That way there's someone in front of the door."

"You're safe from the Devil if there are people there to protect you?"

"Yes."

"Then we're very safe here. Did you see all those police officers outside? I get it, you know, that if you actually went to a place, you saw the Devil, and skeletons, and they poured blood on you . . . I get that you're very scared. But there are a lot of police officers outside. There's no way the Devil is getting in here."

Instead of trying to understand how a ten-year-old girl could be so paranoid, Dr. Roccia seemed to be feeding her fear. "I'm sure that the Devil won't get you. I spoke to many children who told me many secrets. They were afraid of being killed, or of disappearing. I spoke to a girl who was scared to death, but then nothing ever happened to them . . . The grown-ups told them, 'If you tell anyone, the Devil will get you,' but nothing ever happened."

I listened to these exchanges in my kitchen with my headphones. I almost choked on my coffee several times. Those videos seemed to come from a parallel dimension, where reason and good sense were alien concepts. "I know that someone hurt you in the bottom or wee-wee. I know because the doctor [Maggioni] told you. Do you feel like talking about how someone obviously hurt you in the bottom or wee-wee? Take another piece of paper and try to draw what happened to your wee-wee."

Margherita had talked about touching. But the psychologist insisted. It couldn't have been just that. They must have done more. In the end, Margherita gave in. They raped her. Questions like these showed that there was a diabolical mechanism at play, which explained a lot. The results from the gynecological exam were being used to induce the children to talk, even though for months they repeated that nothing had ever happened. It was only later, during the trials, that other doctors determined that Margherita showed no "sure signs" of abuse, but by then it was too late. Like all the other children, she'd become afraid of her entire family.

"What did you think when they took you away from home?" Dr. Roccia asked her.

"At first I didn't get it, but then I found out that they were doing certain things to me, and I thought, *Good thing they took me away.*" She didn't remember. She'd found out, probably through techniques for the forced recovery of latent traumatic memories similar to those used during the American Satanic Panic.

"Good thing they took you away!" Dr. Roccia said. "I would have said to myself, 'Ahh, what a relief!'" What right did an expert witness have to make such a comment about the girl's family? It was beyond comprehension.

In another video, Margherita was sitting with Alberto Ziroldi, the judge for preliminary investigations in Modena. She was telling him about how she was taken to the cemetery in the evening and how the Satanists ordered her to recruit other children by telling them that "a wizard wanted to meet them."

The judge looked a bit shocked. "Where did you go to find other children in the evenings?" he asked.

"I found them in the yard."

"How did you find children in the yard in the evening? Children are usually home by then."

"Yes, but I knew these children," responded Margherita, unfazed. "They asked their parents for permission, and then they came to meet up with me."

Despite the obvious absurdity of this answer, Ziroldi didn't press her. He changed the subject. Margherita was recorded again when she was twelve years old, responding to the questions of a juvenile court. The video was dated March 2001, three years since she'd last seen her parents. Her features had changed. Her rounded, youthful face was now longer. She was wearing a black, red, and white checkered shirt. She was smiling. She was much more confident, more aware. She was very happy where she was, she said. With Lara and Giovanni. Her saviors. She had no desire to go home. Quite the contrary. She also wanted the judge to take away her nieces and nephews, the children of one of her older sisters. She said she no longer felt anything for her family. As far as she was concerned, the case was closed.

I stopped to think; I was consumed by doubt. Margherita had clearly told a completely distorted story. After her father's conviction in Modena, the Court of Appeals in Bologna and the Court of Cassation hadn't believed her and had acquitted him. But I still didn't understand. If Margherita and her family were so tight knit, as her parents and siblings claimed, how could their relationship be severed so completely, and in such a short time? How could that pure, visceral connection born in the uterus and developed during those first steps and those first games—the simple act of being together for thousands of nights and days—dissolve as if it had never existed?

I often thought about my children and what united us. To my very core, I couldn't believe that everything my wife, Debora, and I were building during the crucial years of their childhood could be so easily shattered. The very thought that this could happen terrified me. I couldn't believe it. I consulted various experts in legal psychology, some of whom had followed the case closely or participated as expert witnesses. Almost everyone agreed that anger was a key driver of the children's radical change in behavior. They also suggested that the children had experienced a deep sense of disappointment caused not so much by the idea of sexual abuse but by the feeling of being rejected and abandoned by their families. Which is exactly what Dario had said during our brief encounter.

It made sense. The trauma the children experienced when they were taken away must have been violent. One morning, they'd woken up in their bed, in their room, in the place that until that moment had been their home, their town, their school, with their friends, their passions, their sports. Then suddenly, that very night, they were catapulted into an unknown family, another bed, with other rules and dynamics. And then to another school, with other teachers and other classmates.

Seven, eight, ten years of life undone in the time it takes to go from breakfast to dinner. A world where there was nothing to hang on to, a world devoid of any reference points. Where had their family gone? Why weren't their parents looking for them? Why weren't they coming to get them? Their place had been taken by a woman. A doctor. Who, from the very first minutes of meeting her, used such strange and scary words. *Problems. Safety. Protection.* Veronica, Lorena's daughter, put it nicely when she told the judge how Dr. Donati had justified taking her away from her family. "They immediately told me, 'You're safe. Now we have to understand from what,' because I hadn't said anything yet."

Judge Ziroldi asked her to clarify. "OK, so you asked yourself, 'But from whom do I need to be protected?' 'Why do I have to be protected?' Did you ask yourself that? Did you ask anyone?"

The girl shrugged. "I wondered it in my head, but, I mean, it was like I couldn't find the answer. Valeria (Donati) and I started to make sense of it together when I started to talk."

Even faced with such glaring clues, Ziroldi hadn't investigated further. He'd changed the subject.

"Valeria told me that you find it hard to place children in foster care, and that you struggle," Margherita told a juvenile court in her last recorded interview. "But I think it's good that you do it, because, OK, even though you don't know what problems they have, you really helped me. I couldn't wait to leave that family, because they were hurting me. I'm very happy about this."

The Giaccos lived on the second floor of the projects on Via Volta, in the same building from which the Gallieras had been evicted. When I got there, Santo was in the courtyard unloading a few crates of oranges from his van. He had white hair, a white mustache, and the yellow teeth of a man who'd spent his life smoking. I followed him upstairs, to a three-bedroom apartment full of pictures of his six children and twenty-three nieces and nephews. Pictures of Margherita were everywhere. There were snapshots of her as a little girl, and the hall was covered in recent pictures that someone had managed to download secretly from her Facebook page. The kitchen window was fogged up from the steam coming from the boiling pot of pasta and the bubbling tomato sauce on the stove. Maria was wearing a thick white-and-blue robe. Margherita's room had remained the same since the day she was taken: salmon-pink walls, orange closets, a caterpillar and a butterfly on the headboards of the two twin beds where two stuffed animals, a teddy bear and a lion, were sitting.

Maria collapsed to the floor in tears. "Can you bring her back to me? Even just for half an hour. I want to see her before I die!"

While I was talking to Santo in the living room, she grabbed my recorder from the kitchen table and left a message for her daughter. I only noticed it later. "We talk about you every day, Margherita, *'a mamma*. They told you lies, come home. I think about you day and night, *'a mamma*. Don't you ever think I'll forget you. My love. I miss you. I don't want anything from the law. I want my daughter."

Santo was forced to close his construction business due to the time he spent in prison and on house arrest before his acquittal in 2001.

The family's finances were hit hard. His children watched, powerless, as workers from a furniture company walked into their house to take back furniture purchased on installments. They watched Maria's hysterical fits. She'd suddenly found herself without her husband and without her youngest child.

"We thought she'd gone funny in the head," said Antonella, one of Margherita's older sisters. "One time we even had to call the ambulance and have her put in a straitjacket."

When the trial was over, Santo went back to working as a mason, but then he started to "do the markets," selling fruit. Things weren't going well.

"How did your father treat you?" I asked Antonella when we were alone. "Like royalty." He never harmed them, never did anything strange to any of them. And Margherita was untouchable, "or else." She was the darling of the family. Loved, wanted, very spoiled. "At nine years old, she still took her milk from a bottle" at breakfast and before bed. Maria gave it to her in secret, because Santo didn't approve. "What's this? She's all grown up and she's still drinking from her baby bottle?" When she was taken away, her mother descended on social services with a box full of Margherita's things, begging them to "give the baby bottle to the girl, or she won't sleep."

The Giaccos were a humble family, very affectionate. The house was a meeting place for family members who came, went, drank coffee, smoked cigarettes in the kitchen, and then left. But all those people and all those children couldn't ease the pain that had fallen on that house in the spring of 1998.

A few years later, Antonella found her sister's foster family and called her. Margherita was distant. She asked why, if her family really cared about her, no one had even tried to find her before.

"I told her we couldn't. None of us could do anything," Antonella told me. Her sister said she'd always been told the opposite, that no one had ever come looking for her, and that her parents had died in a car accident. When Margherita turned eighteen, Antonella went to look for her in person, but the girl said she wasn't interested in reconnecting.

Maria was obsessed with the memory of her daughter. She burst into tears more than once during my visit. Santo would scold her with a hint of the sarcasm he employed to keep the rest of the world at arm's length. But his indifference was feigned. When we were alone, sitting at the kitchen table, he looked me straight in the eye.

"Tell me the truth," he said. "Did you see my daughter?"

"Yes."

"How did she seem? The house, everything OK? How was she? Was she pale?"

I hadn't noticed. And I didn't see the house. When Alessia and I found her—on the outskirts of a town an hour away from Massa Finalese—she hadn't let us in. She'd leaned out the second-floor window over an internal courtyard. She listened to us from there. We explained that we were looking into her case and that there were some things we wanted to understand. She wasn't interested. She wanted to be left alone.

"I see," said Santo, resigned. On the kitchen table was a pack of cigarettes, a lighter, and an ashtray. And something I hadn't noticed until then. Maria had pulled it out for me. It was a cassette titled "Cemetery inspection." I found an old tape player. The A side contained some old Queen songs. The B side was the recording of some people in a car. Three men's voices: inspector Antimo Pagano, baritone; prosecutor Claudiani, shriller; and a person with a strong Neapolitan accent, Carlo Marzella, deputy prosecutor for the district anti-Mafia directorate in Palermo. There was also a woman's voice with an Emilian accent, Valeria Donati, and the voice of a little girl, Margherita. They'd taken her to identify the locations where the rituals had taken place.

"You choose where you want to go," said Claudiani.

"Straight," said Margherita.

"Can we go to the cemetery?" asked Dr. Donati.

"Yes," said Margherita.

"Can you show us how to get there? You remember our deal, right? If you don't want to go anymore, if you're scared, you can tell me. Otherwise, we won't be able to understand."

Once at the cemetery in Finale Emilia, they asked her if she wanted to get out of the car. Margherita was terrified. She wanted to stay in the car. She pointed to some locations she remembered.

"Is there any particular place that reminds you of something?" Marzella asked.

"That one."

"This bridge? Why, what did you do there?"

"They killed some kids there, and we danced. We did all those ugly movements with our clothes, then . . ."

"How did they kill the kids?"

"With that bolt. I don't know . . . the one for chopping off heads . . ."

"This happened during the day or at night?"

"When it was dark out. Then on the grass over there. There, if I remember it right, they dug up some kids, and they put some other kids in."

"Do you remember who was there when these things happened?"

"My dad, all the kids, sometimes my mom."

Then she named a priest.

"Giulio . . . Don Giulio."

"Who?" asked Claudiani.

"Gio . . . ," said Marzella.

"Umm . . . Don . . . Hold on . . . Don Giorgio!"

They'd corrected her. The girl had talked about Don Giulio, a name she'd already mentioned before multiple times. But Marzella suggested the "right" name to say. It wasn't the first time Don Giorgio's name had come up in this strange way.

Margherita's foster father was also one of the first to suggest Don Giorgio's name to her. One evening, after she had returned home from a session with Dr. Donati, he'd taken her aside. Lara talked about it at the trial. "It was clear that they'd been pressing this issue for a while. My husband kept asking, 'Come on, at least tell me what letter his name starts with.'" They'd gotten as far as *G*. "He rattled off a list of names: Giovanni, Giuseppe, Giordano, Gelsomino. And then he said, 'Giorgio.'" And that *Giorgio* is what stuck. Even though sometimes she said Giulio. It didn't matter. Maybe because it was already decided that Don Giorgio Govoni was the head of the sect. Even though there was no proof.

The police had initially been suspicious of Don Giorgio's search history. But prosecution experts later determined that it was of no relevance. *Girl*, *hard*, and *friends of children* weren't code words related to the world of pedopornography but acronyms for animal rights organizations, technical components of the computer itself, or sites that dealt with adoption.

No matter. The prosecution had the children's testimonies. They had Cristina, who'd come to the same conclusion with the help of Dr. Avanzi, who'd studied religion under Don Giorgio and who'd even had her daughter baptized by him. They'd also played the name game with *G*, as Dr. Avanzi herself later admitted in court. "At first I said, 'Giuseppe,' so she said, 'Gian.' So we started with *Gianmarco*, *Gianantonio*, *Gianvittorio*. Everything with *Gian*. And we could have gone on for a while. Then she started to say, 'I'm sick. My tummy hurts' . . . Finally she stopped, and all of a sudden said, 'Giorgio. Don Giorgio.'"

19.

One day in October 1998, around the time when things were really heating up and several other children were starting to confirm Dario's cemetery tales, Valeria Donati met with Melania, a five-year-old girl from Mirandola. Melania and her brother, Marco, had been taken away due to their parents' substance abuse problems. Their mother, Roberta, was working her way through a program aimed at getting her children back. Dr. Donati met with the children on a weekly basis to monitor their development and progress.

Melania arrived with her foster father. He took Dr. Donati aside to tell her about something concerning that had just happened. He and Melania were flipping through a magazine together. "We were looking at pictures of Lake Maggiore, and she asked me whether the person who'd taken them was still alive, or if they had died." The question must have shocked him. "In the moment, it left me speechless. Of the many questions a little girl could ask, that is certainly not one of them." Dr. Donati stepped up the visits. "From that moment on, in particular, I remember that during the week, Melania said to me that she'd also been taken to cemeteries and that she'd experienced abuse there . . . She said, 'I have to tell you something important.' She wanted me to go to her room with her, and that's when she burst into tears."

Then Melania told Dr. Donati that she'd seen her mother slit a boy's throat. Roberta lost custody definitively and was indicted in the Pedophiles-2 trial. She then became pregnant with a third child. An AUSL psychologist in Mirandola noticed her belly during one of their meetings. "Ma'am, do you know that we're going to have to take that baby, too?" Terrified, Roberta ran. Not abroad, like Lorena, but just a few miles away, to Lombardy. Giada was born at five a.m. on November 18, 1999, in a hospital outside Mantova. At around nine a.m., the head physician called Roberta to his office. They sat down. "Ma'am, someone from social services in Mirandola just called. They wanted to know if you'd given birth. Can I ask what's going on?" Roberta burst into tears and told him. The doctor listened in silence. Then he said, "Don't worry, I'll take care of it." Instead of releasing her from the hospital two days later, he kept her in for a whole week, the time she needed to initiate proceedings with another juvenile court. After a few meetings, they allowed her to take her baby home with her. Despite acquittals on all three counts, she was never allowed to see Melania and Marco again. They were taken away for good and placed with different families.

Giada grew up as an only child. When she became old enough to learn the details of her mother's story, she decided to find her brother and sister. But they never accepted any of her Christmas or birthday presents. They never replied to any of her messages on social media.

"But I never had anything to do with this. What did I do to *them*?" she asked me when I met up with her. After years of silence, she'd accepted the idea that Melania and Marco would remain strangers for the rest of her life. But not the idea of having to pay for something that wasn't her fault.

Sunday in Salernes is market day, and the Cours Théodore Bouge teems with people sitting at Café des Négociants or wandering around stalls full of flowers, Provençal lavender, and aged cheeses. One Sunday, I walked through it with Stefano Covezzi. He was smiling and nodding to friends and acquaintances. Salernes has a smaller population than that of Massa Finalese, the town his mother had escaped to keep him—her fifth and only remaining child—from being taken away along with the others.

At almost eighteen years old, Stefano was a handsome young man with blue eyes and thick eyebrows. Growing up, Stefano noticed that his family was hiding a dark past. His father didn't always live with them. He went back and forth between France and Italy. Lorena sometimes ran off to Massa Finalese to visit her family, and when he was little, she rarely took him with her. Although she was affectionate and attentive, Stefano noticed that she never interacted with other children, as if she felt uncomfortable around them. And someone had mentioned something about his uncles being in jail. Something strange was happening. Something unsaid. Until one day Lorena told him the truth. He had four siblings, but they'd been taken away from her because of abuse that never actually happened. Since then, they'd dedicated a few prayers to Veronica, Pietro, Federico, and Aurora in their nightly rosary. Stefano couldn't understand why his siblings didn't want to come back to their mother and father. Or why they'd always refused to meet him or to have any kind of relationship with him.

"My parents are incapable of hurting anyone," he told me in Italian marked by a heavy transalpine accent.

"I know they would have raised my siblings in the same way they raised me. I think that someday I'll have to be the one to introduce them to my mom."

Meanwhile, some of his French friends had searched his name online and found several articles containing the word *pedophilia*. Stefano had been forced to explain his strange story to them. Lorena talked about it as little as possible. She wanted to lessen the effect of her history on her son and preferred to keep her memories to herself, venting only to her husband or to close relatives. But in 2013, Delfino, "the good father that never yelled at" Stefano, died of a heart attack, leaving the two of them even more alone. Stefano wanted to support and encourage his mother more than ever, so he started going with her to public events regarding her children's cases.

As Stefano was growing up in Salernes, his brothers and sisters, spread out across different families, were going through the difficult and painful process of examining the nightmare that had changed them forever.

I couldn't understand the deep cruelty behind the social workers' decision to separate siblings. Then I found a report from the juvenile court in Bologna with statements made by Dr. Donati and her colleague Anna Maria Gemelli. Dr. Donati had recommended separating the four Covezzi children, claiming that it would be impossible to find a foster family that could look after them all and "also maintain a high level of protection," especially after a sudden, urgent removal of minors on whom "we didn't have any information." She'd assumed that Lorena and Delfino were criminals from the get-go. But the main reason for the separation was that Dr. Donati and her colleagues wanted the four children to remain apart, "because clearly . . . a family or a community that takes on (only) one, has a level of attention and ability to read signals that is different compared to one taking on four . . . so it was also a calculated choice, also derived from experience . . . And then later it turned out to be a fitting choice." Isolating each child from their parents and siblings would allow Dr. Donati and her colleagues to study them better. And none of them, according to her, seemed to be the least bit interested in returning home. Quite the contrary. From the moment they were plucked from the waiting room of the Mirandola police station, all the children seemed relieved that they were being placed with new families. They didn't seem to want to see their brothers or sisters again.

Dr. Donati, Dr. Gemelli, and social worker Maria Teresa Mambrini subjected the children to an intense schedule of meetings. But for four months, none of them accused their parents of anything. None of them remembered anything serious or traumatic happening at home. But the doctors insisted. In a report by the Bologna juvenile court, Dr. Gemelli explained which words they used to try to convince the Covezzi children to report their parents. "Talking to the judge is the same as telling Mommy and Daddy how much you're hurting. Make them understand how much you're hurting, and if your parents understand this, they might even understand you, and they might change."

Then, in March 1999, Dr. Donati approached Veronica's foster father after one of her sessions. "Dr. Donati took me aside and told me that Veronica was really hurting, and that she thought she might soon confide in us. And in fact, as we drove home, I realized Veronica really was a bundle of tears and tension." And one at a time, they began to talk. Their statements were filmed for the preliminary investigations. Lined up together, they looked like a string of vague and contradictory accounts.

Veronica loved her uncles. She said she got along with them well. But then she accused them of taking her into the countryside, blindfolding her, and doing things to her "down there" with a metal object.

"My uncles would release my arms, let me put my clothes back on, and put me back in the car."

"Have you ever been to a cemetery?" asked Judge Ziroldi.

Veronica answered as if it were the most natural thing in the world. "Yes! To see my relatives."

"Did you ever go at strange hours of the day?"

"Can you repeat the question?"

"Have you ever been when it was closed?"

"No. I went with my grandmother or my aunt, or with my cousins, always around eleven thirty or twelve o'clock."

"So never at night?"

"No."

This blatantly contradicted everything her cousin Cristina and the other children had said about nighttime rituals. But soon after, Veronica's memories returned. Yes, she'd also been late at night. They also did the Black Masses in the middle of the afternoon, "toward four thirty p.m., five p.m.," right after school.

Veronica was plump, with curly hair and a raspy voice. Likeable. Affable. Polite. Chatty. She wanted to cooperate and give investigators all the information she could remember. Although Pietro looked so much like her—they were both the spitting image of Delfino—he had a very different personality, maybe because of the two-year age difference. When he spoke, he seemed either bored or distracted, or he snickered, or he chewed gum. I had the distinct impression that he was testing them to see how far he could go before Dr. Roccia and Judge Ziroldi would stop believing him. As if that meeting, which would determine the fate of his entire family, was just a big game. "Uncle Emidio turned off the lights and dressed up as a black devil, with blood coming out of here"—he pointed to the corner of his mouth—"you know, like that stuff they sell in the shops. It's red marker. Then he'd put his dentures in . . . He said he'd take out our hearts, take out our eyes."

"And when did you find out it was him?" Dr. Roccia asked him, stupefied.

"I took off his mask, and that's when I found out." The following day, he repeated the same tale, but this time claimed that the masked uncle was Giuseppe, not Emidio.

"I pulled off his mask, so he grabbed me and started to hurt me . . . with a bamboo stick. He made me take my shirt off, and he beat me on my back."

"And then?" Dr. Roccia asked, urging him on.

"He was punching me in the face. Kicking me in the face."

"And were your parents there?"

"They weren't there that day."

"And when you went home, your parents didn't notice anything?"

"No . . . Then the next morning it was all gone."

Dr. Roccia seemed speechless, but she chose not to press him further.

"Was Uncle Giuliano there, too?" Judge Ziroldi asked.

"No," Pietro answered, effectively clearing his uncle's name by contradicting Cristina's version.

When he was feeling talkative, Pietro would list all the tools his uncles and their associates used to torture him. For example, they tied him to a cross and threw knives at him. He also confessed to an impressive number of murders of and episodes of torturing unidentified minors. But the game of tall tales was gradually altering his perception of reality, transforming it into a grotesque horror movie where he was the main character and everyone wanted to kill him. He slid into a spiral of anxiety and paranoia. He had to be repeatedly reassured that the police were standing outside the door. Multiple times, as with Dario and Veronica, he claimed to have seen his parents or other shady characters lurking around his new town. He'd even asked to be moved. When his sister invited him to her confirmation at her parish, he said he was afraid the place wouldn't be "protected" enough.

The psychologists admitted to having instilled in the children a fear that someone would go looking for them. When questioned by the judge, Dr. Gemelli said, "We told the children that the others had also been contacted. We wanted them to remain vigilant." They hadn't considered that the warning itself—relating to unproven facts, no less—had triggered the children's fear of persecution.

Over time, the four Covezzi children began to manifest rising levels of distress. Spontaneous crying, hysterical fits, and violent outbursts. Federico, the youngest boy, was giving his foster parents an increasingly hard time. They often found his room in disarray, as if he hated everything that surrounded him. Meanwhile, Veronica and Pietro felt a deep sense of guilt toward their younger siblings for having been forced to sexually abuse them. For a while, little Aurora—still locked up in the Cenacolo Francescano while waiting to be placed with a foster family—hadn't wanted any contact with them.

"Aurora, what did you do with Mom, Dad, and your brothers and sister?" asked Dr. Sabrina Farci, one of the psychologists from Turin, during a closed-door hearing. They were sitting on the floor, playing with a dollhouse.

"I don't know," said Aurora, focusing on the toys around her. She'd just turned four.

"I don't know . . . ," repeated Dr. Farci. "This is a way of saying, 'I don't want to talk about it.' I think you do know. Maybe it hurts you to talk about this. Do you feel like talking about it?"

"Nope."

"Then I won't be able to help you, Aurora."

But in the days that followed, Aurora accepted her help and began to answer her questions.

"I don't understand why you don't want to go home anymore."

"Because Mommy and Daddy hurt me."

"What did they do? Can you tell me?"

"No."

"Why not?"

"They spanked me in the behind."

They eventually found a new home for Aurora. She grew up far away. Lorena never saw her again, not even in a photo. I wasn't able to find her, either. But Alessia and I tracked down Veronica and Federico. They both listened as we explained why we'd shown up on their doorsteps out of the blue. They were both still living with their foster families, and they weren't interested in reliving events from the past. The same went for Pietro. I reached him by phone in the northern European country where he was living. It was all water under the bridge as far as he was concerned. Their father's death hadn't upset any of them. And they didn't want to have anything to do with their mother.

The same went for Cristina. For her, the past was scorched earth, a land she had no reason to return to. Her mother had died in prison, and she was terrified of her father, Giuliano, and her uncles. The foster family that had taken her in when she was eight years old hadn't managed to hold on to her for more than a few months. She was messy, unaccustomed to cleanliness, and too difficult, too complicated, too hysterical. She'd completely disrupted the life of her foster mother, Gilda, and terrorized Gilda's younger daughters with tales of dead people and cemeteries. Gilda couldn't let her stay. And she was done putting up with those psychologists who reminded her every time Cristina visited them: *Be very careful when you leave here. When you leave neuropsychiatry, be very careful that you are not followed.*

So, with a lump in her throat, Gilda explained to Cristina that maybe they weren't the right family for her, and that she'd be happier somewhere else. Social services found her another family in the province of Imola. Giovanna and Simona, eighteen and sixteen, respectively, would be her new sisters. But their brief experience with Cristina was so negative that when Giovanna was finishing her degree in psychology years later, she chose Cristina as the subject of her thesis. Social services had told Giovanna and Simona's parents about the children from the Bassa Modenese who'd been abused by their families. Their parents suggested they welcome one of these children into their home. The girls were excited by the idea of having a little sister or brother to look after.

They were assigned Cristina, who arrived on December 7, 1999. Giovanna and Simona greeted her with a pair of black velvet pants and a light-gray top they'd bought especially for her the day before.

Cristina had been described to her new family as "a nice little girl, studious, diligent, curious, cheerful, likeable, and affectionate." But their efforts to help her settle in "were constantly foiled by two of Cristina's repeated strategies: throwing tantrums and crying fits like a three-year-old, and telling lies, misbehaving, and acting up like a thirteen-year-old," as Giovanna wrote. Soon, Giovanna, Simona, and their parents realized they were dealing with a deeply unstable person.

> **Cristina lived in her own world, where she dreamed and fantasized and pretended she was a Barbie. But she had no grasp on reality. She often tried to take our stuff, our personal belongings. She often told us things that weren't true. She told on my sister and me for things we didn't do. In school, she had a spoiled relationship with her classmates. She moved quickly through friendships, telling people many different things about herself, some true and common among her peers, some dark and probably untrue. This led her classmates to distance themselves from her. She seemed to prefer the company of adults anyway, but for utilitarian reasons: because of their role, adults could and had to give her more attention, and especially presents. Her relationships were primarily of convenience, and she would pull away if she didn't get what she wanted. My sister and I didn't see her as a sister, just as a little girl who made our parents fight and tired out my mother or any adult who looked after her. She was a liar who told macabre stories in the bathroom every morning (probably some of my memories of this time were compromised by suggestion), who blamed us for things and who didn't care about us.**

It was a crude analysis of what Cristina and some of the other children had become after they were taken from their families.

> **What I disliked the most about this whole affair was the behavior of the social workers, the psychologist, and the educators . . . They led Cristina to believe**

> **that we were the wrong family (as with her first foster family and her birth family), and that she wasn't at fault in the least. They even gave her the idea that she could change families at will, until she found the right one. This mode of operating was, I believe, damaging to her, as well as to us, and after reading up on the subject, I now know that it's also morally and methodologically wrong.**

Giovanna believed that the statements Cristina had made to the psychologists and judges fell under the category of "latticed allegations," which often accompany group contagion. "A unique feature of latticed allegations is the high number of interviews psychologists impose on the children in order to extract more information."

On October 10, 2000, less than a year after arriving at Giovanna's house, Cristina was assigned a new family, and Giovanna never heard from her again. I wasn't able to find out much about what happened to her after, other than that she ended up in another region and that she'd gone to college. I found myself rereading the letter she'd written to the judges in the fall of 1998, a few months after being taken away, when she was still with her first foster family. Together with her statements, that letter had dismantled the Morselli and Covezzi families. It had ended with that appeal: "If my parents and uncles start to say that the things I say are true, be a little bit nice to them, but until they tell the truth, always stay harsh."

A lot of things about that letter didn't make sense. It didn't seem to have come out of the head or hand of an eight-year-old girl. Why would she take the initiative to reach out to a judge? What is the meaning of the sentence "I will tri [sic] at all costs to make myself remember who those people were"? If words and terms have specific meanings, what exactly did Cristina have to "make [herself] remember"?

"The passage where she writes 'I will tri [sic] very hard to try to understand' is particularly jarring," said Daniele Amistadi, a systemic psychologist, in an interview. "If the abuses in question had occurred, Cristina would have them clear in her head and wouldn't need to work to understand something she experienced firsthand. Moreover, the expressions she uses are often not in line with her age. The document could have been written under dictation or, anyway, under the guidance of an adult."

A few months after I contacted them, Veronica, Cristina, Margherita, and Melania sent me a letter through a lawyer in Florence. In it, they defended the work of Dr. Donati and her colleagues and attacked whoever believed they'd been taken away from their families for no reason. "We can assure you that there were plenty of reasons, and we're happy to have been taken away from them. They made us suffer for many years."

20.

During our conversation, Gloria Soavi, the president of CISMAI, rejected any criticism of her organization. Legal psychologists had accused it of creating "abusologists"—psychologists and social workers who tended to look for signs of sexual violence in children who showed any hint of distress.

"CISMAI—not then, not now—is absolutely not in favor of finding abuse where there is none," she told me decisively.

However, in some of the more famous cases of suspected pedophilia, CISMAI psychologists seemed to have used that exact approach. As if a child's testimony should be considered valid no matter what—regardless of how it came about. CISMAI is also a partner of the International Society for the Prevention of Child Abuse and Neglect (ISPCAN), whose home page reports incredibly alarming statistics without noting where they come from. One claim is that "one in four girls . . . is a victim of child abuse." According to these numbers, the average elementary school class contains at least four girls who have been abused.

Marinella Malacrea has been among the top authorities in Italy on abuse and violence against children since the 1980s. She is also a founding member of CISMAI and of CBM in Milan. She has consulted for prosecutor Pietro Forno, written academic articles on the subject, and participated in numerous conventions alongside Claudio Foti, the founder of Turin's Hansel and Gretel Research Center. She is a fierce enemy of the authors of the *Carta di Noto*. Dr. Malacrea has also been holding training courses since the 1990s, some of which were attended by Dr. Donati. Because Dr. Donati was fresh out of interning when Dario told her his first stories, she called Dr. Malacrea and asked her to supervise her work.

"A careful and thorough job," Dr. Malacrea said when I asked for her opinion on Dr. Donati's work. A job that was "very good, emotionally present, just as the circumstances required."

Dr. Malacrea believes that a psychologist's true challenge when working with child victims of abuse is their impenetrable silence. She called it "one of their most effective tools for evading a question or pretending they didn't hear it." But the idea doesn't seem to take into consideration the possibility that the reason they're not saying anything is that nothing has happened to them.

Dr. Malacrea told me that contrary to what is reported in Italian and international scientific journals, it is "highly improbable" that a psychologist could negatively influence a child, because "it is very hard to instill in a child's mind something that could compromise their life." If the children still talk about beheadings in cemeteries, crucifixions, cat blood, murders, and rapes after weeks of visits, those statements "could stem from the imagination of the abusers or from fiction, from the set design . . . used to market products that are distributed around the world. Pedoporno-horror films—a genre we know very well exists and that the postal police have their hands full of—require a fair amount of staging."

This explanation seemed a bit patchy to me. I thought it improbable that anyone could rely on "set design" to trick so many nine- and ten-year-olds into thinking they were in a real cemetery and that they'd dug up real corpses or that they'd killed real children. And it's absolutely not true that the postal police "have their hands full of" pedoporno-horror films. Three agents from the most important centers for the fight against pedopornography in the north, center, and south of Italy confirmed it. They've been monitoring video material that circulates around the world for the past twenty years. None of them have ever come across a snuff movie with a satanic background, human sacrifice, or the drinking of blood.

Forensic psychologists aligned with the *Carta di Noto* continue to clash with CISMAI over which methods should be official when listening to children. Time, experience, and new cases—like those that hit the Abba and Sorelli nursery schools in Brescia and a nursery school in Rignano Flaminio—were starting to increase awareness of the risks of using interrogation methods that were not neutral and impartial. "For this reason, more and more consultants are refusing to respond when judges ask them whether abuse occurred," explained forensic psychiatrist Marco Lagazzi. "That can and should only be established by the judge. All we can do is provide a psychological profile and evaluate the child's ability to give testimony. Or to verify that their testimony of a given event hasn't been distorted by pressure or suggestion. Nothing more."

Translated into the words of Chiara Brillanti, a legal psychologist who worked as an expert witness in the Modena trials, "The psychologist must be the psychologist. They cannot be the police officer. They should not push the children to talk. They have to be a neutral figure. There was nothing neutral about these psychologists [in the Bassa trials]."

Oddina Paltrinieri thought it was all about the money. She said it often. People had profited from those children—the foster families and especially the social workers and their superiors at AUSL. They were so certain they'd discovered the case of the century. They built an entire network around it, generating a ton of work, from consultancies with prosecutors and judges to training courses and research grants.

I didn't know whether I agreed with this interpretation. Though I thought it was improbable that a bunch of pedophiles, who typically have mental health issues and act alone, had all randomly found themselves living in two towns in the Bassa Modenese, I struggled to accept the idea that so many psychologists would construct a case out of thin air just to make money.

A clerk from the Mirandola town hall sent me an email with a report from the Union of Modena Towns, North. It listed expenses for foster families, which included protection and care for the removed children. The data was impressive. The total amount of public money spent on the case—excluding the five trials—was around $4.5 million. Of this, the smallest amount had gone to the foster families, who on average received $650 a month per child, and who therefore didn't make any money from their actions, despite what many believed. But more than half the budget had been dedicated to "psychological cures" alone. This was an ambiguous line item, to say the least.

While she was working as a contract psychologist for AUSL in Mirandola, Valeria Donati also started to run an independent facility in Reggio Emilia where she was assisted by Dr. Gemelli and social worker Maria Teresa Mambrini. It was called Centro Aiuto al bambino (CAB), the Center for Helping Children. In 2002, the regional health board assigned "the treatment and therapy of children involved in the case to CAB, as it has the tools and expertise needed to deal with matters of abuse."

The same person who had discovered the case, treated the children, gathered their initial statements, chosen their foster families, reported to the prosecution and juvenile court, acted as a key witness in the trials, and always discouraged contact with biological parents—even after they'd been acquitted—was also reaping potential career and economic benefits for her central role in this whole affair. For each child,

Dr. Donati's center received between $1,250 and $1,700 per month, depending on the seriousness of the case. Over the course of about ten years, CAB received $2.7 million in public funds, despite the glaring and potentially dangerous conflict of interest. If the psychologists had restored contact between the children and their biological families, CAB would probably have lost its funding.

I tried to understand how this could have happened. As I delved deeper into the story, I wrote to, called, and visited many of the people who, at the time, thought the defendants really *were* guilty: the prosecutors in Modena, the juvenile court in Bologna, members of the police force. The rare responses I received were brief and evasive. A few words to essentially say *no comment.*

I never understood the mental mechanisms that led so many experts on this case to see what was invisible or unimaginable and completely miss everything that was right in front of their faces. Maybe I never will. They never questioned their assumptions. They carried on believing that this story went in only one direction despite the mountain of clues and warnings that pointed the opposite way. They focused on the words coming out of the mouths of babes. But after having run the gamut of the same experts, these children all gave similar versions of a story, and they all developed strong paranoia and anxiety even though they'd been promised that talking would free them of the weight they were carrying. How did this happen? I'll probably never find out. But after years of research, Alessia and I came to the conclusion that once the assumption of guilt had been established, it would have been very difficult to backtrack and admit even the smallest error. Thus, a small, sordid story of presumed pedophilia was blown out of proportion and transformed into something that swallowed up everything and everyone in its path. Families were torn apart and children were traumatized. And five people were dead.

When I searched for Valeria Donati in order to ask her for an interview, I found out that after having worked at CAB in Reggio Emilia for many years, she'd transferred to another center in Modena. A visitor to her office told me it contained rooms with toys, presumably for children in therapy. A colleague of hers confirmed that the center provided expert witness services to courts in Modena, Reggio Emilia, and Ferrara in the years following the trials of the Bassa. When I asked Dr. Donati for an interview, she replied:

> **I have a deep respect for the pain and privacy of these families, especially for the boys and girls. They are now men and women struggling to rebuild their lives after facing enormous hardship and suffering. For this reason, even though I would like to express my opinion on a few general points, and to clarify information that was revisited or distorted by time, I never even considered the idea of doing it publicly or through the media, not even when I was unjustly attacked.**

I tried to contact her a few more times, both over the phone and in person. I wanted her version of events. No deal.

The only person who would meet me was Marcello Burgoni, Dr. Donati's former superior at social services. He welcomed me into his house in Mirandola. He's a mild-mannered and polite man with gray hair and a gray mustache who is long since retired. We passed through a hall and an internal courtyard to get to his dining room. He offered me a seat at the table, but he didn't sit down. He remained standing and leaned against a cabinet. I felt his nervousness. He told me that at the time, none of his social workers or anyone among the police or judges had any experience with that type of case. It was the first time for everyone. His responsibilities were limited to gathering testimony and providing evidence to the court, which then chose to act independently. The social workers weren't the ones who'd decided to remove the children. It was the judges. I challenged him. The juvenile court had acted based on warnings from his office, trusting his opinion and that of Dr. Donati.

"Dr. Burgoni, why did all the children who came through your office tell such strange stories?"

Dr. Burgoni opened his arms. "I've asked myself that same question many times. I've never been able to answer it."

I didn't understand so I pressed on.

"Do you really believe that these rituals in the cemetery happened?"

Dr. Burgoni shook his head. "I don't know. I don't know. I have no idea, actually."

I was baffled. This man had put a young and inexperienced psychologist on a case that required specialized knowledge and a high level of professionalism. He validated her work. He was present during the majority of the removals. He read the protective orders out loud to crying parents, suspending their custody because they were suspected of having taken their children to cemeteries for sexual and satanic rituals. But the children had never said a word against their moms or dads. And now he didn't know whether to believe the stories?

"Now, hold on," he said, correcting me. "A child was removed after they said they were abused at home, not before."

I stopped him right there. This was false. Demonstrably false. It was all in the reports, in hundreds of pages of transcripts from the hearings and trials. The children themselves had said so to the judge. I listed all sixteen children, one by one. All torn from their families without a shred of evidence. Dr. Burgoni shook his head.

"That's enough . . . That's enough because I don't think . . . It seems that the conditions aren't there to . . . The story was built and rebuilt by the trials, and that's it now, and it can't be otherwise, because that's the truth now."

But the trials hadn't just convicted people. They'd also acquitted them. In many cases. What truth was he talking about? Did he still believe that his psychologists' methodology was appropriate?

"The methodology was legitimate at the time. In the sense that they were the first experiences."

"So you could have gotten it wrong?"

"No one is infallible . . . No one is infallible."

I asked him to explain why and by what logic all those brothers and sisters—the Scottas, the Covezzis, the Morsellis—had been separated. But by then, Dr. Burgoni had buried his head in the sand. "I'm . . . I can't go on."

He wanted me to leave. He was feeling "threatened." Before I left, I looked him in the eye. "Do you know in your heart that you didn't ruin those children's lives?"

Dr. Burgoni swallowed hard. He put one hand to his mouth and opened the door to his house with the other, asking me to leave. The evening air was cold. I walked for a long time before getting back in my car.

21.

On Thursday, July 26, 2018, at ten twenty-five a.m., I was waiting at a traffic light on a provincial road outside Padua when I felt my phone vibrate with a WhatsApp message. When I read the sender's name, I almost had a heart attack. It was Marta. I pulled over immediately. The cars behind me honked in protest. But my senses were numbed.

"Hi, Pablo. I don't know if you still have my number, but you contacted me about that investigation into the cases in and around Mirandola. I'm sorry I sent you away. The thought has been bothering me because I think you're right. I've always had my doubts."

I think I reread the message five or six times before driving off again. Of all the children who'd been taken away and whom I'd tracked down, Marta was the one I probably thought about the most. Her story had deeply upset me, as had her mother's tragic suicide. I often wondered how an eight-year-old girl had withstood the impact of such a tragedy. After she arrived at the Cenacolo Francescano, her past had been completely swept away. She was the last person I was expecting to hear from.

The following morning, Alessia and I went to Reggio Emilia with a trunk full of reports Marta wanted to see. She wanted to know everything Dr. Donati had said about her, and she wanted to read Dr. Maggioni's medical report. We met up in a parking lot outside town. The shy little girl in a red sweater I'd seen in the videos with the judge's consultants was gone. She'd become a beautiful young woman with wavy hair and a bright expression.

"You are the absolute first people I'm speaking to about this thing," she told us when we got in the car. "My boyfriend doesn't even know."

"Not even your friends?" asked Alessia.

"No one knows. I've forgotten a lot of things about that time. But I'm one hundred percent certain that I made everything up. The story I told the social workers, the psychologists, the judges . . . Those things never happened to me. I think someone put words in my mouth . . . It certainly didn't come from me."

We looked at each other in silence for a few seconds. Those "words" had been used to obtain prison sentences for the Gallieras and Federico Scotta. And now, with difficulty and courage, Marta saw them for what they really were: garbage.

"So many times I thought, 'That's enough, now I want to tell them I made everything up.' But then the mind goes to when you were little, to the judges, the courts . . . and in that moment I thought no, I mean . . . I don't want to go through all that again."

She only had a few faded memories of her previous life, which she spoke about with detachment, as if those first years with her mother in Mirandola had never really belonged to her. She could barely remember Francesca. "She wore glasses, she had long black hair . . . Fairly thin . . ."

After Francesca died, Marta had asked Dr. Donati many times if she could have a photo of her, but no one ever gave her one. "Do you have one by any chance?" I told her that her brother, Carlo, had many, and that if she wanted, I could put her in touch with him. When I mentioned his name, she didn't react.

"Why did you call me?" I asked her.

"I want to get to the bottom of this story and understand what happened to me. I want to go to the psychologists and social workers, tell them to look me in the face and tell me that they have no doubts about what they did . . . But I think it will be very hard to get answers from them."

Marta didn't remember much about the morning of July 7, when the police showed up at her door to take her away. She remembered her mother crying as the officers searched the house. The only fragment of memory she had was of "someone who wanted to get me, and I bit them . . . but as for everything else, dark . . . dark . . . I . . . know that I was very, very close to my mother, because in the end, let's say that she was the only one there, and Mom is Mom, so yes, I'm sure I loved her very much, even though . . . she wasn't a saint, in the sense that . . . Well, sometimes she could be a bit aggressive, a bit quick with her hands."

She remembered an episode in which her mother slapped her and chased her with a slipper. But her stay at the Cenacolo was a jumble of freeze frames. Like the time her mother had gone looking for her, and she'd glimpsed her through the fence.

> **I remember hearing a voice calling me, so I immediately recognized her even though I actually couldn't see her very well because there were some trees or bushes in the way, and . . . Well, I don't remember my reaction very well . . . I mean, I don't know if I was happy, sad . . . Probably a bit of happiness, a bit of anxiety . . . but I think I immediately went to the nun to say, 'Look, my mom's here!' . . . I remember that she gave the nun a doll with a backpack, and . . . inside was a letter. I don't remember what was written on it, but something like 'I love you, I'll be back soon,' or something like that. But then I never . . . I never saw her again.**

In the meantime, Valeria Donati had come into her life. They began a series of visits that were "never-ending, exhausting . . . I have flashes in which I was resting my head on the table and wanted everyone to stop talking, because they were constantly saying, 'Tell us what happened to you. If you tell us, you'll feel better . . .' And initially, I didn't know what to tell them, because I knew that nothing had happened to me."

Contrary to what Dr. Donati had implied during the trial, Marta had asked her if and when she could see her mother again. "She always told me that it wouldn't be possible to see her again . . . Because she told me some ugly things and . . . that we first had to resolve this issue and then, maybe, after . . . But then this after never came."

Marta had few memories of her medical visit with Dr. Maggioni. After examining her, Dr. Maggioni had told her, "Someone hurt you. If you want, you can talk about it," as mentioned in the report from the hearing I showed her. Marta shook her head. "I didn't believe it, but what could I do? How could a doctor tell lies?"

Marta always remained conscious of the fact that she'd made everything up. But even so, she grew up with a lingering doubt about what had really happened when she lived with her mom, causing her no small amount of confusion.

"I thought about it a lot over the years. I also thought about things that are probably absurd . . . That they'd drugged me . . . That maybe my memories disappeared and came back again. I mean, for example, I searched for 'rape drugs' online." It was the only way she could make sense of the possibility that all those horrors had disappeared from her memory.

A few days after her visit with Dr. Maggioni, the psychologists called Marta into a room at the Cenacolo.

"I only remember that they said, 'Your mom is gone,' and I said, 'Oh, where did she go?' 'No, it's not that she left—it's that she's dead,' and then . . . I don't remember anything else. But I remember that I cried."

Odette Magri, a social worker, told the court she'd told Marta, "This thing happened because her mother understood, after her exam, after she'd been taken away, that everything was out in the open now. There was nothing she could do, and she probably thought that she had no way out." The completely biased interpretation of an expert who'd already decided, a priori, which truth Marta should subscribe to for the rest of her life.

"I always carried this doubt with me, too," said Marta. "I mean, if my mother knew she was innocent, that she didn't do anything, why did she jump from the fifth floor?"

After Francesca's death, Marta's visits became even more frequent. Dr. Donati wanted to know if Marta knew Dario, if she could confirm his stories. But Marta had never seen him. She'd never been taken with him to "the house of a priest who raped them." What priest was this? She didn't know anyone in Massa Finalese. Dr. Donati didn't believe her. "You should know that he gave your name . . . so you were there . . . You were in that situation," they repeatedly told her.

"I remember . . . a table. I was sitting on one side, she on the other, like in an interrogation . . . They made me draw so much. I probably wanted to draw, too, because I knew that if I was drawing, I didn't have to talk."

Then, exhausted, she gave in.

When Marta was about ten years old, social services found her a foster family. She went to live with a couple in their fifties with adult children. But things started off badly with Emma, her new mother. The woman was "always very cold." Their relationship was tense from the beginning. No hugging, no expressions of affection. Only fights over millions of little things. Emma often called Marta a liar and reminded her of how "lucky" she was that they'd kept her. Some of the other children had bounced from one family to another. "My foster mother never really made me feel like a daughter."

Marta spent her eighteenth birthday at home looking out the window. CAB had warned her: now that she was an adult, she had to be careful. They might come looking for her. They. Them—the bad people whom she and the other children had locked up in prison and whose lives they'd ruined. Her anxiety lasted a few days. Then Marta came back to her senses and started to think about the future. She had no idea what she wanted to do, but she liked children. She'd become a teacher.

If I hadn't been looking at her throughout our meeting, if Marta had only been a voice, I would have thought she was telling me someone else's story. I detected no trace of pain in her tone. She was completely detached, as if her past had become a little dot in the universe, a star that was light years away from her. No hesitations, no anger. She was the same girl who, twenty years before, sitting in front of a psychologist, wearing a red sweater, had talked about being abused as if she were going through her homework. All my questions, no matter how heavy or hard, bounced off her without fazing her in the least. Her answers showed the reflexes of someone who'd talked about the matter hundreds—thousands—of times to pretty much anyone. Not those of someone talking about them for the first time, at the age of twenty-nine, in a parking lot outside Reggio Emilia, with the only strangers who might be able to understand the nuances of her senseless story.

I got the impression that she'd just emerged from a long and deep emotional hibernation. It had probably preserved her sanity but numbed her feelings toward the people who'd loved her and cared for her as a child. She didn't miss her brother, Carlo. He was a stranger to her. She had only a vague memory of him. He hadn't been there for important events in her life. She didn't feel like seeing him again. Every time the conversation touched on her mom, she didn't show any particular emotional reaction.

But her eyes were speaking a different language. They betrayed an emotion and a sense of powerlessness that she seemed to have been able to contain—but not to eliminate. And it was probably growing within her now that she was an adult, surrounded every day by schoolchildren and their mothers who dutifully picked them up every afternoon.

I didn't know if I should ask. I hesitated a lot, and I felt like an ass for doing it. "If it hadn't gone the way it did, if your mother was still alive, would you go back to her?"

For the first time during our long conversation, Marta seemed confused. "I was hoping you wouldn't ask. Because I don't know . . . Maybe I would . . . maybe I would . . . Maybe, if she was alive, I might have the desire to see her, maybe even from afar. Even without asking her anything or saying anything."

When I called Carlo to tell him about my meeting with his sister, he was silent for a few seconds. "Oh, God, I feel sick." Then he pelted me with questions. "How is she? What did she say? Do you think she wants to see me?"

I lied. "I don't know. Maybe."

22.

It was a Sunday morning in early May, and Daniela Roda was shuffling around her three-bedroom unit on the ground floor of an apartment complex north of Finale Emilia, doing housework: the washing, the dishes from the night before, the floors, the litter box. Daniela had a hard time getting going in the morning. It was the effect of the powerful benzodiazepines she took in the evenings before going to bed. The chemicals induced an artificial sleep that helped her get through the night. Otherwise, she'd wake up with a start and find herself sobbing into the pillows three or four hours before her alarm was set to go off. And they helped her keep her mind off her daughter, Sonia. There was a framed picture of her on a cupboard in the kitchen. It had been shot just before they took her away in the fall of 1998. Sonia was standing tall, with long, stick-straight brown hair and green eyes, looking shyly at the camera.

Daniela was focusing on the thousands of chores she struggled to get done every week, so she didn't immediately realize that the house phone was ringing. No one called the landline anymore aside from sales reps looking to sell her something. She'd only kept it so she could hang on to the thread that tied her to her daughter. She was sure that if Sonia wanted to find her one day, she'd remember that old number. But now she didn't know whether to answer. Who could it be, on a Sunday morning?

"Daniela Roda?" It was a young man's voice.

"Speaking."

"Wait one second," said the man. "There's someone here who wants to talk to you."

A woman's voice came on the line.

"Mom, it's me."

It was Sonia.

Daniela felt faint. She let herself fall onto the couch. The shock completely floored her. All she could do was sob. She didn't know what to say, what to ask. Sonia broke the ice. One of her daughters had a problem with her eyesight, and the doctor wanted to know if it was hereditary.

They exchanged goodbyes, promising to see each other sometime. Daniela gave Sonia her cell phone number and then found herself checking her phone obsessively with a mixture of euphoria and fear that her daughter would disappear again.

Daniela's sister was Monica Roda, Giuliano Morselli's wife and Cristina's mother. Before she was taken away, Cristina and her cousin Sonia would spend afternoons together at their grandmother's house while Monica and Daniela were working. They were only one year apart, and they were very close. They usually played with Barbies and drew pictures. Sometimes Sonia would get annoyed with Cristina for copying her. Sometimes they both spent the night at their grandma's house. They'd share a bed, laughing and telling each other stories until sleep overtook them. Other times, Cristina would spend the afternoon at her aunt's house, where Daniela treated her like a second daughter.

At the time, Daniela was living alone with Sonia in Finale Emilia after an ugly divorce. She and her ex-husband also had an older son who lived with his father in Massa Finalese.

Then, in July 1998, Cristina disappeared. Sonia didn't fully understand the meaning of the word *removal*, but she knew that something very scary had happened to her cousin. Several months later, Cristina accused her father's entire family of sexual abuse, including Giuliano's brothers and his sister Lorena, along with her husband and their four children. Cristina told investigators that her cousin on her mother's side had also been present in the cemeteries. Her father, Massimo, would take her there at night. She said he belonged to the gang of Devil-worshipping pedophiles. On November 12, 1998, as the police descended on the Morselli and Covezzi families, a squad car went to Massimo's apartment to arrest him. Another showed up at Daniela's house to take Sonia away. They woke them up at around six a.m. Daniela went to the door to find men in uniform and a social worker standing outside.

"Ma'am, we have to take your daughter away."

"What do you mean, take her away?"

Sonia was still sleepy. She recoiled from the sight of so many people. She started to cry.

"Ma'am, calm her down because she's very agitated . . . Prepare a bag for her with a few things."

Daniela panicked. "What do you mean, a few things? Where are you taking her?"

A female police officer went into Sonia's room to check on her as she got dressed. Then, holding back tears, Daniela placed a backpack on her daughter's shoulders and promised her that she'd pick her up that very evening. But a few hours later, at the police station in Mirandola, Marcello Burgoni from social services handed her a ruling suspending her custody. Outside, Daniela ran into Lorena and Delfino. Everyone was incredulous. They didn't understand how their niece, so fragile, so insecure, had unleashed such chaos.

Daniela and I met a few months before Sonia's surprise call. She was exhausted and shattered by pain. The hope of even just hearing her daughter's voice again was weakening with the passing of the years.

Sonia's closet contained a few toys, school notebooks, and a black planner, its red bookmark stuck on November 12, 1998. The homework assignment for the following day was written in block letters: *STUDY GREECE.* I found one of Sonia's essays in a drawer. It was about a trip she'd taken to a town near Mantova. Her handwriting was neat and precise. Daniela burst into tears. I found myself sitting on the floor, consoling a woman I'd only just met.

The doorbell rang. It was Maurizio, Sonia's brother. It was incredibly hard for him to relive the story. He talked so quietly that he almost whispered. He often paused to dry his tears.

He and Sonia loved each other very much. After he came of age, he and Daniela turned to a private investigator, who'd tracked Sonia down in Reggio Emilia. She was living with a lawyer and his family. But not just any lawyer—he worked for the Cenacolo Francescano. Maurizio went to look for her and ran into her outside her house. Sonia seemed happy to see him. He showed her pictures of his newborn daughter. He'd named her Sonia. He gave her his number. "Mom and I are waiting for you, whenever you want to come back." But in that very moment, Sonia's foster mother leaned over the balcony and gestured for him to leave. He hadn't heard from her after that.

But now here she was, that shy little girl, reemerging from the shadows after a long absence that had drained all the joy from that house. She was now a grown woman, and a mother of two daughters. Daniela didn't have to wait long after that first phone call. Sonia sent her a message almost right away. "Mom, it's me, this is my number." It didn't seem real. Twenty years had passed since she'd heard her daughter call her that. And now she'd just heard it twice in ten minutes. Soon after, she and Maurizio were embracing her in the middle of a shopping mall. All three of them had the strange feeling of having just said goodbye the night before.

"Then we sat down at a table to talk, and she pulled a picture from her wallet," Daniela told me. "It was of us when she was a little girl . . . Then and there my heart told me, 'This girl never forgot you, never, never, never . . .' I'm her 'mommy' again, I can have her close to me again."

They had a lot to talk about.

A few months later, Daniela wrote me a message. "Sonia asked me for your number. She said she wants to talk to you." I met Sonia on the second floor of a residential building outside Reggio Emilia. She was a woman of few words. She'd spent her entire adolescence in silence, suffering because she was far from her loved ones. She'd become a mother for the first time at twenty-three years old. It changed her perspective, and she began to wonder if her mother was still waiting for her. The psychologists had torn her mother to pieces over the course of the years, instilling in Sonia the belief that she was evil or dangerous. But she never needed her mother as she did in that moment.

"I missed her from the day I gave birth to my first daughter. I found myself alone, in the birthing room, with no one, with a six-pound daughter in my arms. I didn't even know how to change her diaper. That's when I understood . . . how much I missed her . . . I missed her in the small things, in the advice on how I should dress the baby . . . what I should do if this happens or that happens. I mean . . . they seem like such stupid things, but . . . I had a void."

Since the morning of November 12, 1998, no one had ever shown her that kind of love. As with Marta, Sonia had foster parents who were much older. "They were cold, unfeeling. He was seventy-seven years old, and she was sixty-four. I felt like an object, plucked from one place and taken to them."

On the threshold of thirty, Sonia had come to realize that she'd been the victim of a kidnapping. For a long time, she'd felt a muted bitterness toward her psychologists. Now it burst forth into a veritable fire. "I remember everything that happened to me . . . everything. I want to see these people removed from this environment. They shouldn't have anything to do with children. That's all I ask. I don't want anything else—no excuses, no money, nothing. I don't give a shit. I want it for today's children, because they shouldn't have to experience what I went through."

After the police arrived, Sonia was taken to a center in Forlí and then placed in a foster home. She was expecting her mother to pick her up that evening. But she didn't know that if Daniela had looked for her or even approached her, she risked being arrested.

Her father, Massimo, was detained and ended up among the defendants in the Pedophiles-2 trial. He was sentenced and then acquitted at the Court of Appeals and the Court of Cassation. Unlike the other children questioned by the psychologists and judges, Sonia never talked. She didn't accuse anyone. She denied everything. The rapes, the cemeteries. Everything.

Daniela was never implicated in the investigations, yet she was required to attend meetings with a psychologist tasked with evaluating the parents involved in the case. As with the other parents, the psychologist hinted that the only way Daniela might be able to see her daughter again was to admit her knowledge of the abuse. Daniela denied everything. Massimo may have been a terrible husband and an absent father, but he'd never done anything like that to his daughter.

Meanwhile, Sonia had started the process of meeting with Valeria Donati. Dr. Donati hadn't wasted any time. "She told me that my mom wasn't good because she wasn't protecting me, that she practically agreed to let my father do those things to me, abuse me, take me to cemeteries. My mother was covering for him." Sonia denied it, either with words or with long, uncomfortable silences. She understood soon enough that *nothing happened* was not the answer the doctor was expecting.

Her cousin Cristina had made some very serious accusations that required immediate intervention. There was no question of seeing her mother again, at least not while Sonia insisted nothing had happened. "I was supposed to forget about her . . . I wasn't allowed to see her until I told them what the other kids were telling them."

But Sonia continued to resist. Even when Dr. Donati and Ms. Benati prepared her for her exam with Dr. Maggioni. "They told me that if she didn't pull out her camera, then everything was fine. But if she took pictures, then I had to worry. Because it meant that there were signs of abuse."

This was a lie. Pictures are always taken during examinations of suspected victims of child abuse, because they become evidence. The doctor had taken pictures of her private parts. There were signs of abuse. And who cares that a consultant at the trial expressed strong doubts on the matter. Dr. Maggioni had said it, and that was enough. "At every meeting, they reminded me that the exam spoke volumes, so it was useless to keep quiet. The signs were clear anyway, so there was no doubt. It was certain."

We were sitting on her couch as we spoke. Sonia sometimes went silent and quietly cried. It was no lament, just tears streaking down her face. "I was telling them that none of it was true. I didn't care about what Donati said or what Maggioni said." That's when the doctors' behavior turned more hostile. "They told me that I was a liar, that I was a coward, that they knew the truth . . . because the other kids had already told the truth. Pure and simple psychological violence, that's what it was. I mean, she talked for an hour a week, for four and a half years, to a little girl who was crying . . . Unperturbed, she carried on with her narrative. Anything I said was of no importance."

Dr. Donati wanted to know about her relationship with Cristina. What did they do together, where did they go, who did they see? Sonia told her that she sometimes went to her house in the countryside outside Massa Finalese, where her uncles had a barn with some tools. And where they played with some kittens. "Valeria kept saying, 'We already know that the cats were tortured in front of you at night in the cemeteries. They killed them, and they made you drink the blood.'" If she couldn't remember those horrible things, it was because her parents had brainwashed her to make her forget. Sonia kept silent. She kept asking to see her mom, but she was told there was no way.

On March 22, 2000, a year and a half after she'd last seen her mom, Sonia was summoned to judge Eufemia Milelli for a closed-door hearing.

"Listen, Sonia," said the judge, "do you know who I am?"

"Yes."

"I'm a judge. And do you know what we have to do today?"

"Yes."

"How old are you?"

"Eleven."

"Let me ask you this: Would you like to go home to your parents?"

"Yes."

"Who do you want to go to?"

"To my mommy."

"Do you have good memories of your mom?"

"Yes."

"You're sure of this?"

"Yes."

"Do you think that what Cristina said was right or not?"

"I don't think so."

"Why not? Tell me about it."

"Because nothing ever happened to me. My parents never did anything to me."

"Did your dad ever take you to strange places, not normal places for children?"

"No."

"No, or you don't remember?"

"No."

Even that hadn't been enough. They kept her locked away and barred her from seeing her family. The following year, the juvenile court in Bologna wrote a report in which it called Sonia a "little collaborator." Her behavior was deemed unacceptable, akin to that of children raised in Mafia families. Desperate, Daniela came to realize that the only way to see Sonia again would be to go to Mirandola's social services and declare, "I can't rule out the possibility that my daughter was sexually abused."

Three years later, they allowed supervised meetings in the presence of Dr. Donati. They could only occur under a specific condition: "We couldn't talk freely. I couldn't ask certain things, like we couldn't look to the past," Sonia told me. "I couldn't show any feelings, emotions, or thoughts. I mean, I was afraid of thinking because I thought they could read my mind. We couldn't be spontaneous, to talk. It was very sad."

Daniela's little girl was behaving like a stranger. Sonia didn't look at her, and her answers to Daniela's questions were monosyllabic, as if she were afraid of her. And she was. After three years of separation and incessant questioning, Sonia had come to the conclusion that it would be dangerous to go home. She'd been led to believe that her mother would prostitute her. Especially now that she was older. That teary woman in front of her reminded her of all the pain and loneliness she'd had to endure. Their monthly meetings continued even after Sonia was released from the center in Forlí and transferred to a foster family.

Daniela showed me some videos of their supervised meetings. They were always under the watchful eye of a psychologist. The older she got, the more Sonia seemed to withdraw. Daniela talked to her, brought her presents and clothes, but her daughter's body language communicated strong discomfort. She was always sitting with her hands between her crossed legs. Her answers were short. During their last visit, just before Sonia's eighteenth birthday, Daniela told her that now they could meet anywhere they wanted. But Sonia shook her head. "I don't think so." They hadn't seen each other since.

Soon after, Daniela Cassanelli, Dr. Donati's colleague at CAB, learned that Maurizio had shown up outside Sonia's house and given her a picture of her newborn niece along with his phone number. She immediately told Sonia that the picture was a fake, a pathetic attempt to win her back. She shouldn't fall for it. She convinced her to throw it away and delete the phone number from her phone in front of her.

It took Sonia years to decide to reach out again. It took her years to realize—once and for all—that she'd lived two-thirds of her life apart from the only people who had ever truly loved her.

December 2018

Carlo returned home around dinner time. He was angry. He'd spent the afternoon fighting someone over the phone, and he was in a terrible mood. He didn't feel like seeing anyone or doing anything. He threw himself on the couch and looked at the ceiling. He planned to spend the evening alone, channel surfing and trying to quell his rage. Then he heard the doorbell ring.

Due to the dark and the fog, all he could see was a shape at the gate.

"Who is it?"

No answer.

"Well, who is it?" he insisted, perplexed, as he crossed the entryway. Then he saw her: a pretty girl with wavy brown hair. His sister. Marta. He threw his arms around her and cried. She was crying, too.

They went into the house. He took her to the attic and showed her their mother's old box of things. They looked at pictures, and Marta cried again upon seeing the album Francesca had prepared with care after she was born, gluing in pictures of her, one by one.

It would take her some time to get used to having a brother again. They both knew this. For now, all that mattered was that they'd seen each other again. After twenty-one long years.

I was sitting on my bed that evening. It was late. My children, Yasmine and Sebastian, were asleep in their room. I was resting against the headboard with my computer between my legs. The phone on my nightstand started to vibrate. It was a video call. It was Marta and Carlo, together. They just wanted to say hi. I had no words.

After the call, I spent half an hour staring into nothing. For the first time in many years, I cried, too.

July 2021

This book was published after the release of *Veleno*, a podcast that my colleague Alessia Rafanelli and I created between 2015 and 2017.

After the series and book came out, things started to happen. The story appeared on numerous Italian television networks, and in the summer of 2019, the district attorney's office in Reggio Emilia arrested several psychologists and social workers. They were charged with removing children from their families for financial gain on the basis of false accusations of sexual abuse. The Hansel and Gretel Research Center in Turin, the nonprofit organization that employed Dr. Cristina Roccia and Dr. Sabrina Farci—the psychologists who interviewed the children from Mirandola and Massa Finalese—was at the center of the investigation.

Claudio Foti, the center's founder, was convicted in November.

In an interview from June 19, 2021, in *Il Resto del Carlino*, an Italian newspaper, Valeria Donati said she no longer works as a psychologist and that she had received death threats since this story had come out.

Sonia's and Marta's statements led Federico Scotta to request a retrial to clear him of all charges after eleven years of prison and after his three children were taken away. The Ancona Court of Appeals denied his request, which they deemed inadmissible. The Court of Cassation also rejected Federico's appeal. In the meantime, he found his son, Nick. He hadn't seen him since he was six months old. Now they are very close.

Four years after Dario and I met outside his house, he reached out to me again. He wanted to get in touch after that last message in which he urged me not to come near him or call him again.

He explained that his adoptive mother, Mrs. Tonini, had found out about our meeting and instilled the fear of God in him. She was convinced that the sect of satanic pedophiles was still trying to sniff him out. Her obsession with this line of reasoning had caused him significant psychological distress. He'd had to check into a mental hospital on two separate occasions.

Then, one day he decided he'd had enough. Dario wanted to see his birth family again. At thirty years old, he left his adoptive family. Soon after, he was embracing his brother, Igor, and sister, Barbara, again, telling them he always knew that they were innocent and that their father, Romano, and mother, Adriana, were, too. Unfortunately, his parents had already passed away. But others who'd known him and loved him as a child were still there waiting for him with open arms. Giulia and Claudia, Oddina's daughters, and Silvio, their father, welcomed Dario back into their home, the same one where he had lived for three months when he was three years old, before being taken to the sisters at the Cenacolo Francescano.

When he arrived, Dario was weak, skinny, worn-out. Over the next few months, he gained weight, stopped taking medication, and decided to start a new life.

Mrs. Tonini was unforgiving. "You have to choose," she wrote to him in a WhatsApp message. "Us or them."

Dario's response was unequivocal. "I want to live my life."

ACKNOWLEDGMENTS

I want to thank Alessia Rafanelli, journalist and travel companion in this long affair that led us to become coauthors of the audio series *Veleno*, released in eight episodes on repubblica.it. Her contribution, her tenacity, and her hard work were essential to this investigation.

Thanks to Gipo Gurrado (music and sound design), Marco Boarino (artistic direction), and Debora Campanella (research and editing), the team behind the first seven episodes of the podcast.

Thank you to Luca Micheli, musician, sound designer, and radio program director who alerted me to this story and assembled the eighth episode and set it to music. His wife, the writer Sabrina Tinelli, suggested the title *Veleno*.

Thanks also to the Visual Desk of *La Repubblica* for having supported and published this project.

All the research that went into *Veleno* wouldn't have been possible without two people who are no longer with us: Oddina Paltrinieri and Don Ettore Rovatti. Their extraordinary efforts to gather documents and testimony guided us throughout. I want to thank them both. Rovatti's book, *Don Giorgio Govoni. Martire della carità, vittima della giustizia umana*, was an invaluable text.

Thank you to the family of Oddina Paltrinieri—her husband, Silvio Panzetta, and their daughters, Giulia and Claudia—who helped me a lot during my research, welcoming me into their home over the years and allowing me to access their archives. Thank you also to Antonella

Diegoli—schoolteacher in Finale Emilia and a parish member of Don Ettore—who gave us the same level of support.

Thank you to Patrizia Micai, one of the attorneys who followed this case from the very beginning and who helped me navigate the legal system, an unfamiliar terrain for me. She dedicated countless hours to this project, despite her many other commitments. And thank you also to lawyers Pier Francesco Rossi, Cristina Tassi, and Guido Bomparola for being at our disposal.

Legal psychologist Chiara Brillanti, who consulted for the defense, also dedicated long and invaluable hours to explain to me the various aspects of this affair. I wouldn't have understood them without her. Along with her, I'd like to thank child neuropsychiatrist Giovanni Battista Camerini, forensic psychiatrist Marco Lagazzi, psychologist and lawyer Guglielmo Gulotta, psychologists Angelo Zappalà, Rita Rossi, and Corrado Lo Priore, and Professors Giuliana Mazzoni and Massimo Introvigne. They all answered my thousands of questions and calls with a great deal of patience.

Thanks go to Antonio Platis, councilor for the town of Mirandola, who granted me access to the reports containing the sum CAB received for caring for the removed children.

Thanks to Paolo Repetti and Francesco Colombo of Einaudi Stile Libero for having believed in this project. And thanks to my editor, Roberta Pellegrini, who supported me, motivated me, and gave me precious advice over the months.

Thanks to my lawyer, Francesca Infascelli, for insisting I work on this book when I was about to give up on it.

And finally, thanks to my wife, Debora, and my children, Yasmine and Sebastian, for patiently waiting for me every time I left home, and for the hugs they gave me upon my return. You are my refuge. You are my everything.

REFERENCES

The following texts were essential to the reconstruction, analysis, and narrative of the events of this book. Hundreds of pages of rulings, transcripts of hearings and videos, social services reports, and juvenile court reports were also used.

Beccaria, A., *Bambini di Satana. Processo al diavolo: i reati mai commessi di Marco Dimitri*, Stampa Alternativa, Rome 2006.

Camerini, G. B., and Gulotta, G., *Linee guida nazionali. L'ascolto del minore testimone*, Giuffré, Milan 2014.

Cortelloni, A., *Pedofilia e satanismo, risorge l'Inquisizione. Quel pasticciaccio della Bassa Modenese*, http://dibattitopubbl.ucoz.com/_fr/0/Cortelloni_Augu.pdf, 2000.

Dury, B., and Weiser, S., "McMartin Preschool: Anatomy of a Panic," the *New York Times*, March 14, 2014.

Goleman, D., "Studies Reveal Suggestibility of Very Young as Witnesses," the *New York Times*, June 11, 1993.

Introvigne, M., *Satanism: A Social History*, Brill Academic Pub., Leiden-Boston 2016.

Neimark, J., "The Diva of Disclosure," *Psychology Today*, June 1, 1996.

Roach, M. K., *Six Women of Salem: The Untold Story of the Accused and Their Accusers in the Salem Witch Trials*, Da Capo Press, Cambridge (MA) 2013.

Rovatti, E., *Don Giorgio Govoni. Martire della carità, vittima della giustizia umana*, Artioli, Modena 2003.

Shales, T., "The Devil to Pay," the *Washington Post*, October 27, 1988.

Smith, J., "Believing the Children," the *Austin Chronicle*, March 27, 2009.

Steffenoni, L., *Presunto colpevole. La fobia del sesso e i troppi casi di malagiustizia*, Chiarelettere, Milan 2009.

Transmissions from Jonestown, podcast available at http://radiojonestown.libsyn.com/, November 7, 2017.

Zappalà, A., *Abusi sessuali collettivi sui minori. Un'analisi criminologica e psicologico-investigativa*, FrancoAngeli, Milan 2009.

THE BOOK

Children also lie.

And one lie can summon hell.

A legal affair that ruined entire families. A moving story that turned out to be an incredible case of psychological contagion.

At the end of the 1990s, in two towns of the Bassa Modenese separated by a handful of fields and foggy homesteads, sixteen children were taken from their families and transferred to protected locations. Their parents were accused of belonging to a sect of satanic pedophiles who performed nighttime rituals in cemeteries under the aegis of a well-known local priest. The children told psychologists and social workers real-life horror stories. The network of monsters they described seemed endless and involved fathers, mothers, brothers, uncles, and acquaintances. Except there were no adult witnesses. No one ever saw or heard anything. Was the deep code of silence reigning over this corner of Emilia so entrenched as to render everyone untouchable?

When the truth of the matter emerged, it turned out to be just as terrifying as the lies. For many, it was already too late. But someone, maybe, might get a second chance.

Note: nothing in this book was dramatized in any way by the author.

ABOUT THE AUTHOR

Photo © 2021 Michela Piccinini

Pablo Trincia has worked as an award-winning correspondent and writer for print media, TV, and the web. In 2017, he and his colleague Alessia Rafanelli wrote the podcast *Veleno*, a highly acclaimed investigative audio series released in eight episodes on LaRepubblica.it. The investigation reopened the case of the Devils of the Bassa Modenese, one of the darkest and most controversial cases the Italian legal system has tackled in recent years.

ABOUT THE TRANSLATOR

Photo © 2021 Bruno Campigotto

Elettra Pauletto translates from Italian and French into English. Her writing and translations have appeared in *Harper's*, *Guernica*, and *Quartz*, while her book translations have spanned a range of subjects, including music, art, and narrative nonfiction. She earned her MFA in creative writing and translation from Columbia University and now divides her time between Italy and western Massachusetts. For more information visit www.elettrapauletto.com.